# So You Want to
# CHANGE
# THE
# WORLD?

Matthews 5::13-16

# So You Want to CHANGE THE WORLD?

## THE POWER OF EXPECTATION

Don Nori Sr. • Patricia King • D.M. Collins
Rob Coscia • Barbie Breathitt • Adam LiVecchi
Abby Abildness • Dorsey Marshall • Doug Alexander
Lisa Jo Greer • Susan East • Jim Wilbur

DESTINY IMAGE® PUBLISHERS, INC.

P.O. Box 310, Shippensburg, PA 17257-0310

*"Speaking to the Purposes of God for This Generation and for the Generations to Come."*

This book and all other Destiny Image, Revival Press, Mercy Place, Fresh Bread, Destiny Image Fiction, and Treasure House books are available at Christian bookstores and distributors worldwide.

For a U.S. bookstore nearest you, call 1-800-722-6774.

For more information on foreign distributors, call 717-532-3040.

Or reach us on the Internet: www.destinyimage.com

Trade Paper ISBN 13: 978-0-7684-3657-0

Hardcover ISBN 13: 978-0-7684-3658-7

Large Print ISBN 13: 978-0-7684-3659-4

E-book ISBN 13: 978-0-7684-9035-0

For Worldwide Distribution, Printed in the U.S.A.

1 2 3 4 5 6 7 / 14 13 12 11

# Contents

# Introduction

## Don Nori Sr.

It is wonderful that so many feel deep in their hearts that they are called to be world-changers. Here is a big and hearty "Welcome to the club!!" You are a part of a worldwide movement of men and women who are committed to the Lord to be used in whatever way necessary to change the world to His purposes.

That is the good news.

But the bad news follows. Most of us are woefully ill-equipped to actually make even a marginal dent in the world-changing process. But don't be alarmed, for it is not actually your fault. What *will* be your fault is if you do nothing to get equipped. Many will repeat the tired arguments that Bible college, ministry school, and faithful church attendance are the ways we are prepared for whatever task is given to us.

Unfortunately, this cannot possibly be true. These methods of preparation have done very little to stem the tide of moral, cultural, and societal disintegration over the past 50 years or longer. The challenge is deeper than most have anticipated, and the solution will cost you your life.

Still want to be a world-changer? True leaders always stand out from the crowd. Real leaders are the first to see. They are first to proclaim. They are first to do what has never been done. True leaders don't hide behind another or wait for approval from a committee. They are true leaders because they see what others do not see and do not fear the repercussions of their actions. These men and women move from conviction, not from convenience or consensus. They are driven by the fresh wind of the Holy Spirit. This Wind carries new possibilities and fresh answers and solutions. They are the first to be accused, the first to be challenged, and the first to be crucified. Their accomplishments are not understood until generations later, if at all. But they have one passion in life—to be pleasing to the One who has rescued them, loved them, healed them, sent them, and called them friends.

But this is as it should be, must be. For the forces of "sameness" are strong. Tradition, especially religious tradition, is well entrenched. Most don't take well to the notion that what they have been doing is at best an old wineskin and at worst wood, hay, and stubble. Vision, creativity, and true spirituality are too easily consumed by the "Black Holes" of insecure folk whose identity is tied to what they have done rather than who they are in Christ. True leaders move forward in spite of these pitfalls and clearly understand the risks. Nonetheless, they go forth with humility and brokenness, but resolve to see, say, and do what the Holy Spirit within them is so powerfully witnessing.

If this describes you, then you are a world-changer indeed. The people of the world await your appearance; nature groans for your manifestation and the prophets of old have seen you from long ago. King David described you thusly: *"As for the saints in the earth, they are the majestic ones in whom is all my delight"* (Ps. 16:3).

# CHAPTER 1

# It Is Your Destiny—Not Your Destination

## Don Nori Sr.

*The wind blows where it will, and you hear the sound of it, but no one knows where it came from or where it is going. So is everyone born of the Spirit* (John 3:8).

When the Lord spoke to me in the fall of 1982 concerning the name *Destiny Image* (the name we eventually called our publishing company), I was as surprised as many others. In fact, the few publishers that I knew at the time were convinced that using that name would certainly cripple the success of the company. But probably none of us realized that by the time the company was 22 years old, the word *destiny* would become the buzzword of much of the Church.

God spoke to me that we were to call our company Destiny Image because we are destined to be conformed into His Image. He is, in fact, our image of destiny. He would transform us into His image as we yielded to Him in all we do.

So *destiny* has a bit of a different meaning to me. For most, destiny is a destination, either Heaven or a specific career or goal in this life. Most teach that destiny is a place, a single goal in time and space, that God intends us to reach in our lifetime. But I want you to consider that God is bigger than a destination. He made us with a greater capacity than one end, one victory, one accomplishment. Our destiny is far greater than a destination. Our destiny is a place in Him, daily responding to the gentle urging of His Spirit, while being changed into His image.

I will reach many destinations in my lifetime. I can accomplish many goals and fulfill many dreams that God has for me. My destiny is to be led by His Spirit, being used by the Lord in many diverse ways over my lifetime.

Is He calling me to preach the Gospel? Then I shall preach the Gospel...until He leads me in another way. Has He called me to start a business? Then I shall do it with all my heart, bringing Kingdom principles into the work-place...until His Spirit nudges me into another direction. Am I an actor, a lawyer, a mom, a missionary, or a plumber? What I do, I do with all my heart, as though I will be there a lifetime, but with the understanding that He can call me away in a moment. Remember, the Wind blows where it wants to.

*The wind blows where it wishes and you hear the sound
of it, but do not know where it comes from and where
it is going; so is everyone who is born of the Spirit* (John
3:8 NASB).

That is not an excuse to simply abandon what I have
done, but it does mean that in whatever I do, I build in such
a way that I can move to another calling while leaving what
I have been doing in capable hands. We are often hindered
from new adventures in Him because we have not planned
for the moment when He calls us away into something else.
When I understand that He is my destiny, my activity will
change as He sees fit; the only permanent thing will be His
life, love, and power flowing through me to a dying world.

## Remember Who You Are

For me personally, this includes building in my heart the
freedom to move on without the fear of losing my identity.
What I have been is not necessarily what I shall be. What I
have accomplished is not what defines me in my heart, for
I am still full of dreams, desires, and expectations. I shall
forever be open to my Lord and shall forever be willing and
ready to do what He wants me to do. My defining moments
are not the sum of what has come to pass, but my defining
moments are in the responses to my Lord to do what I have
never done, hear what I have not heard, and go where I have
not gone before. What I build is up to Him, but what I discover is solely up to me.

Am I content with what I have done? No, I am not. As long as I breathe, I am on a course of new discovery, adventure, and anticipation. It is not what I have to make myself do; it is who I am. I am compelled to love Him, to search out new realities in Him. There may be nothing new under the sun for some; but for me, every day is a journey opening new possibilities, new horizons, and greater union with the lover of my soul.

I know this is not an easy lesson to learn, but it is truly a liberating one. What I do on earth can change often, but I will always belong to Him. I can be a pastor, then a businessman, then a schoolteacher. But I will always belong to Jesus. Who I am is not what I do, nor is it one of the many destinations I reach in my lifetime. I will always belong to Jesus.

It is disappointing that destiny has taken on a definition so earthy, so self-centered, so…human. For destiny has become the calling card of man's personal achievement; the fullness of his personal accomplishments; the culmination of his deep-seated personal ambitions. Destiny only indirectly relates to our Lord Jesus and the incredible passion of our Lord to live His life freely through us. This is the destiny that Jesus died for, rather, rose from the dead for, to have accomplished through the likes of mere human beings like us.

There is no need to struggle though this process. As matter of fact, if there is a struggle, it is a struggle to rest, to cease from trying, to yield to Him who already would do all manner of miracles through us if we only get out of the way and allow Him to move through us. The smell of humanity, sweat, is a stench before the Lord when it is our attempt to imitate or try to do what only He can do. Remember Paul's most powerful revelation: *"In Him we live and move and exist..."* (Acts 17:28 NASB).

We are spiritual people. As such, we see from a different perspective; we march to multi-dimensional orders given by One whom the world does not know and will never understand. We are not concerned with our visibility, vulnerability, or our capability. These are non-issues, for He can and will do all things for the one broken before Him. Let's put that statement another way. *"I can do everything through Christ who strengthens me"* (Phil. 4:13).

*"Trust in the LORD with all your heart and do not lean on your own understanding"* (Proverbs 3:5 NASB).

My heart is forever His. I do not need the clamor of earthy titles, religious ministries, or paychecks from fickle organizations. I am who I am by the grace of God. My identity is in His presence oozing from my innermost being. That is all I need. That is all you need.

## Brokenness Makes Him Ooze

When I was a child, we often visited my Italian grandparents who immigrated to the United States several years earlier. Of course, they brought with them all the customs and traditions of Italian life. I especially loved my grandfather. I would hug him tightly, but my little arms never made it around his "Italian" waist. I loved his smell. My nose was always pressed against his belly, and I breathed in the aroma of his sweater. One night I asked my mom what Grampap smelled like. "I want to smell like him when I grow up." She looked at me a little worriedly as my dad laughed and explained that his smell was a combination of cigar smoke on his sweater, garlic that oozed through his skin, and homemade wine that was on his breath. The aroma of the garlic and wine oozed through his skin because skin is porous.

In the believer's case, aroma pours out of the openings in our skin as the fragrance of the Lord flows out of our brokenness. When a vessel is broken, whatever is in the vessel automatically flows out. The vessel does not need to force it out. The contents, the aroma, will fill the room until everyone knows what is within. If we have to advertise ourselves or speak of our own anointing, then we have a false aroma, a man-made scent that smells as arrogance and personal achievement. Better to have the aroma of His presence be the telltale sign of the work of the Lord rather than our vain attempts at describing our "greatness" to others!

The key to everything in God is brokenness. Brokenness produces a softness toward the Lord and an understanding of the holy work that God is doing with us. This fragrance cannot be imitated. It is recognizable a mile away. Our soft heart toward the Lord always releases mercy and grace. Humility and dependence on Him will draw God's love and power to you as well as cause it to naturally flow through you. And that, my friends, smells very good.

## Two Secrets

The real freedom to fulfill your destiny is in two secrets. First, God has dreamed many dreams for you to live out in your lifetime. No matter who you are, what your financial condition may be, or who you know or don't know, God has dreams for you and you alone. While He was weaving you in your mom's womb, He was thinking about your future, smiling at the plans He was making for you, and constructing you in the precise way necessary so you could live out every dream to its maximum success.

This is not the work of man; it is the work of God who does what He does because of His own motivation of personal love for you. He knows exactly who you are. He knows your circumstances. He knows your fears, your pain, and your confusion. But He also remembers how He made you. He knows your gifts, and they are many. He knows your talents, for they are great. He knows His plan for you because He developed that plan for you personally. He personally intends to fulfill all of it.

This leads me to the next secret.

## Live in the "Yes" of God

Second, your destiny unfolds as you live in the "yes" of God, responding quickly and obediently to the sweet sound of His voice. Even when, especially when, you do not have the faith, say "yes" to Him. Don't doubt Him. Don't argue with Him. Just say "yes" to your Lord, who is calling you no matter what denomination, faith, or non-faith you now have.

I have seen God do incredible things for people in all walks of life over my 40 years of serving the Lord. He has done miracles for apparently insignificant people, beginning with me. He has touched many Catholics, Lutherans, Baptists, Pentecostals, Brethren, Mennonites, Jews, Muslims, and countless others. If you are breathing, He has dreams for you to fulfill. Say "yes" to Him and watch your life unfold in incredible ways.

## Who Is Too Obscure?

Saying you believe in God is not enough. It is one thing to say you believe the Lord and the dreams He has for you; but it is completely another thing to agree with Him as He moves you toward fulfillment. Our problem is that fulfillment is more frightening than we could ever imagine. It involves moving away from our comfort zone and into the unknown waters of purpose.

Many also think that they are not part of what I am talking about. They think that somehow they are too obscure for God to worry about. At some point they developed the notion that they had either sinned too often or made such a bad mistake that God had rejected them. But these are just the lies brought on by our own fears and our own depression and the general feeling we have of our own unworthiness.

I know how you feel. I was there for many years. But there came a time in my life where I had nothing to lose beyond what I had already lost. All my attempts at success, happiness, and fulfillment had failed.

Of course, we would not have to wait that long, but we humans are a strange lot. We refuse to trust God until we are at the very end of ourselves. Only when we have exhausted every human course of action, do we relent and trust the Lord.

Hey, ask me how I know. I am the king of human strength and stubbornness. That is why I am certain that it is by His mercy that I have done what has been done. If the truth be told, I am quite certain that I didn't do any of it, but God accomplished these things in spite of my impetuous rebellion. I have had to repent long and hard on too many occasions to think it happened any other way. My life is defined by grace and mercy. How can I show anything different toward anyone else?

It is clear to me that those who judge and condemn have never seen themselves as they truly are. The words of Jesus continuously echo within me, "Judge not, lest you be judged" (see Matt. 7:1). Whatever I am, I am by the grace of God. This knowledge does not limit my accomplishments, but it certainly keeps me humble and causes me to walk with a circumspect heart knowing that I could fall at any moment apart from Him.

## You Are More Than You Have Become

The more we understand who we are, and more importantly, who He is within us, the more we will begin to see that we are more than we have become…much more. Our viewpoint is limited by our own limitations. But He is inside and He is not limited by anything. He can change the world through you. Really. Keep your focus on His might instead of your failures and see what will begin to happen. Our agreement with the nature and reality of God within will change the world around us. It will open doors, arrange circumstances, grant favor…in short, will pave the way for the complete fulfillment of all we were born to do.

*…Teach me the way in which I should walk; for to You I lift up my soul* (Psalm 143:8 NASB).

## Points to Ponder

1. "We are often hindered from new adventures in Him because we have not planned for the moment when He calls us away into something else." Would you be ready to move on to whatever God wants you to do next? Or is there so much "unfinished business" in your life that your flexibility and mobility are limited?

2. "Am I content with what I have done?" Do you find yourself being too content, too satisfied with your past service to God, rather than anticipating and seeking what lies ahead?

3. "When a vessel is broken, whatever is in the vessel automatically flows out." What aroma flows out of your vessel? What do people "smell" when they are around you?

# Chapter 2

# So You Want to Change the World? Then What Are You Waiting For?

## Patricia King

I often hear things like the following quotes from precious, enthusiastic, and good-hearted people:

"One day, I am going to see my dreams fulfilled..."

"When I finish raising my children, then I will serve the Lord on the mission field..."

"The Lord has revealed to me that I will be a major world-changer and history-maker one day. I am waiting for Him to bring His purposes in my life to pass..."

"When I get financially secure, then I am going to do some great things for God..."

"I have had many prophetic words and visions over the last number of years confirming that I am going to do exploits for the Lord...one day, I will see them fulfilled..."

"I am not ready yet to yield my heart completely to God, but maybe one day I will..."

## Talk + Action = Accomplishment

Well-known, accomplished world-changers and history-makers did not merely speak about their vision and dreams, but they fulfilled them. Simply having a vision, a prophecy, or a revelatory insight is not a guarantee for fruitfulness and influence. Action is important and vital. Procrastination and excuses are never found in those who create large waves of influence in the earth.

## The Power of Choice

In every believer's heart there is both the invitation and the empowerment from the Lord to be a world-changer and a history-maker for His glory! Few answer the call to its fullness, but everyone can. Your choices in life result in blessing and fruitfulness or lack of them, not only for your own personal life but also for the realms you influence. Every decision you make affects and shapes the world you live in. Whether you use your influence for God or not, you definitely influence people, places, and things. Everyone does! Your choices are creating history—your history. Your choices are also affecting the history of those around you.

During a ministry trip to Thailand, our team had the privilege of hosting a special banquet in order to invite prostitutes out of the bars for the night. We rented a beautiful hotel, ordered the best meal for them that we could, and bought them all flowers. We paid for them to leave the bar for a few hours in order for us to treat them like royalty. We prepared a special program for them, gave each of them a "love word" from the heart of God, and presented each of them with a handcrafted card and a rose. Most of the girls wept due to the deep touch of God's love on their lives. Many of them received Christ for the first time, and a number of them left the bars forever and entered a discipleship program. One of those girls grew strong through Christian mentoring and soon became a fervent prayer warrior, worshiper, and evangelist. It wasn't long before she and a team with her returned to her village in the north and preached the Gospel to all in the village. Many were saved, and she planted a church where the new believers could gather and grow in Christ.

Let's use this example to demonstrate the power and influence of choice. First of all, I made a choice to go to Thailand. While in Thailand, I received a love burden for the girls who worked in the bars. An inspired idea came to mind, and I chose to move forward with it. I returned to the United States with photos and shared the situation concerning the girls in the bars and the inspiration to return and host the banquet for the girls. I decided to receive offerings to fulfill the financial obligation of such a vision. I chose to put a plan of action together for six months later to return to Thailand in order to host the banquet. Many Christians were excited about the vision and made a decision to serve this project in Thailand. They chose to sacrifice both financially and with their time in order to pursue their desire. In Thailand they chose to go to the bars and invite the girls to the banquet. Those who served at the banquet in both practical and spiritual ways chose to do so. As a result of all these choices, many Thai girls chose to receive Christ. Others chose to leave the bars and enter the Christian discipleship program. Those in the program then chose to influence the lives of others through evangelism and church planting.

As a result of all these choices made by many, girls' lives have been influenced for the glory of God, families have been transformed, and entire villages have been reached with the Gospel. It all began with one choice and one person moving in the direction of the leading of the Spirit. That one decision started a chain of events that has changed the lives of many.

## Ripple Effect

You have seen the ripples that are created by throwing a pebble into water. Every day you create "ripples" in life through your words and actions. For example, if you step into your workplace with joy in your heart and a skip in your step, you will influence those in your realm of influence with ripples of joy and gladness. You could change their day to a positive one simply by being happy. On the other hand, if you step into your workplace all miserable and negative, complaining and murmuring, you will also release ripples of influence. This time they would not be ripples of joy but of oppression.

Every day you are an atmosphere-changer or a world-changer even when you do not realize you are. Each day is another day in your history. You get to choose what kind of atmosphere and history you create.

There is power in your choices. Greatness comes as a result of one choice at a time, so be intentional with your choices. Every choice will produce fruit.

## Join the Company of World-Changers and History-Makers

Most individuals today have a life span of about 70-90 years. In the light of all eternity, that is not much time at all. You have the potential to live for the Lord and influence the world around you for good during those years. You have the opportunity to advance the Kingdom of God in your generation and make a mark in time for His glory! Let's look at some famous world-changers and history-makers.

**Martin Luther** (1483–1546) initiated the Protestant Reformation and called believers to live by faith and not by works. His 95 Theses written in 1517 created a crisis and an amazing turning point for the church that we are still enjoying the influence of today. He also, for the first time in history, translated the Bible into the language of the everyday person and encouraged the people to read the Word for themselves. He wrote anointed hymns that are still being sung, enjoyed, and making an impact in the modern-day church.

**William Wilberforce** (1759–1833) was the "breaker" God used to abolish the slave trade in Britain. As a young politician William Wilberforce took great risks to ensure justice and to establish moral foundations in the nation. His acts of benevolence and political reform affected the world.

**Evan Roberts** (1876–1951) was a young man who grew up in a poor family and worked in the coal mines from age 11 to 23. He was limited in academic and economic status but loved the Lord, regularly attended church, and memorized Scriptures at night. He prayed for the nation of Wales to come into revival and it did. He is known today as a catalyst for the famous, nation-changing revival. That revival sparked the Azusa Street Revival in the United States, which launched the Pentecostal movement in America. The movement spread like wildfire to the nations.

**Mother Teresa** (1910–1997) was born in Albania and served as a nun in the Catholic church. She became a citizen of India and served the poor, the sick, and the dying selflessly.

She was internationally famed as a humanitarian and advocate for the poor and helpless. She won the Nobel Peace Prize in 1979 and India's highest civilian honor, the Bharat Ratna, in 1980 for her humanitarian work. At the time of Mother Teresa's death she was operating 610 missions in 123 countries, including hospices and homes for people with HIV/AIDS, leprosy, and tuberculosis, soup kitchens, children's and family counseling programs, orphanages, and schools. Mother Teresa often had audience and voice before kings, prime ministers, and global government, and economic and religious leaders.

These are just a few examples. We could continue and list the likes of Aimee Semple McPherson, Martin Luther King Jr., Dr. Oral Roberts, Dr. Billy Graham, Kathryn Kuhlman, and thousands more who lived in the last century alone. The Bible is also full of individuals who lived for God and obeyed Him. As a result they became influencers for His glory and name's sake in the earth.

## What About You?

The names listed above are well-known on global levels. You might never have your name in lights. Books might never be written about your exploits, and perhaps no one in the earth will ever know who you are or what you have accomplished...but God sees and knows all. As you live before an audience of One, you can influence the world you live in beyond anything you could ever imagine.

You are loved beyond measure. Whether you ever do anything for God's glory or not, you will be forever unconditionally loved. Your worth is never to be measured by what you do or accomplish. Never is your value based on works. You are worth everything to God just because you *are*. You are His treasure and His delight. Your entrance into the world was a significant, blessed event for Him. Your life *is* significant!

You don't *have* to make a mark for His glory in the earth—but you *get* to! Mankind was blessed in the very beginning by God when He said, *"Be fruitful and multiply; fill the earth and subdue it; have dominion over the fish of the sea, over the birds of the air, and over every living thing that moves on the earth"* (Gen. 1:28 NKJV). You do not have to be fruitful and fill the earth in order to be loved, but you will be frustrated if you don't because you were created for this purpose.

God will work on your behalf to fulfill the desires of your heart. You can make your life count for Kingdom advancement. There is no one like you in the entire earth. Just by being born, you changed the world you live in. It would never be the same without you. If you are alive and reading this, you have already made history simply by being born.

## Receiving a Clear Vision

Your actions will ultimately come forth from your vision, and your vision is usually identified or birthed through discovering what you are passionate about. What is your passion? As a brand-new believer I was passionate about sharing the Gospel with everyone I met. I would stay up at night and think of ways I could reach the lost. I was compelled to win the lost. Soul-winning was my passion, my vision, and my life. Every week I won souls to Christ. I was changing their world and their history through leading them to Christ. It all began with identifying my passion, which then birthed vision to reach them.

Have you identified your passion? If so, you will be able to birth vision. If you discover your vision, you are on your way to becoming a significant world-changer and history-maker. Make a list of the things that excite you in life and bring you pleasure. Then make another list of things that feel heavy and negative to you. I always believe that individuals should create a positive, joyful environment around them by engaging in what they love to do. It is helpful to have some things in your life that are a challenge and that do not naturally bring you joy. Those things become your character builders; but for the most part your life should be filled with things you love and activities that create joy in your heart.

I love cooking up a storm, but I do not like painting rooms in a house. I would never choose painting as a career because I feel miserable when I paint and can hardly wait to get finished. Believe me, there is no vision that springs up from within me when I paint except to be finished and to never paint again! I am not thinking of creative ways to paint when I am engaged in painting. I have no passion for painting and therefore lack vision for it.

Cooking on the other hand is different for me. Although I do not have much time to cook anymore, I enjoy it. It brings me pleasure, and when I do cook, my creative juices start flowing. Because I am passionate about cooking, I get vision for new recipes when I am in the midst of preparing a meal. I like trying a little extra spice or changing up an ingredient because vision is unlocked. My passion unlocks it.

I am crazy-in-love with Jesus and love serving Him in anything and everything. He is my passion, and therefore I always find vision in His presence. The more time I spend with Him, the more my passion for Him grows. The more passionate I become, the clearer the vision.

When you make your list of the things that you are passionate about, you will begin to define vision. Focus on those things and dream on!

World-changers have a clear vision that is born out of passion. I had the privilege of spending some time with Dr. Oral Roberts just before he went on to glory. He shared that one of the reasons he had such a fruitful life and ministry was because he was passionate about his "Sacred Time" (the personal time he spent with God). He was so passionate that no one was allowed to disturb him when the door to his prayer room was closed. In that place of his passion God would impart to him vision and mandates. Dr. Oral Roberts stated that when God gave him an assignment in the "Sacred Time," He never had to ask twice. Out of the place of passionate focus, vision was birthed. Dr. Roberts then simply walked out the vision in faith and obedience, and bore fruit. He has gone on to be with the Lord but his fruit remains. He was a major world-changer and a history-maker.

Martin Luther, William Wilberforce, Evan Roberts, Mother Teresa, and other champions throughout history are the same as you. The Bible says that Elijah, the great prophet, was a man like you and I (see James 5:17). All of these world-changers and history-makers simply lived each day following the passion of their hearts in obedience to God. Their passion, their gifts, and the stewardship of their assignments made room for them to influence greater and greater spheres. They were faithful in the little and they were given much. They were willing to lay down their lives for that which filled their hearts with passion—and in many ways, they did. Being a world-changer and a history-maker on that level costs you...oftentimes, everything!

## Plan of Action

Identifying passion and vision is vital, but they cannot stand on their own. A vision without works is just that, a vision. Passion is great and necessary for motivation, but it won't accomplish the assignment. God had passion and vision for the redemption of man before the foundation of the world but He also had a well-thought-out plan of action to accomplish His vision.

Once you have identified your vision, then invite the Lord to give you a plan for walking it out. Start with a vision you have faith for. A weight lifter never starts lifting the heavier weights before he has successfully mastered the lighter weights. If he does not build up his muscles for the heavier weights, he will injure himself. Many in the Body of Christ have been shipwrecked because they bit off more than they could chew and caved under the weight of too large a vision. Begin with small ones. Even small visions when they are fulfilled will influence the world around you.

When I was a young believer in Christ, I had a heart for the aged. I wanted to comfort them and lead them to Christ if they weren't saved. That was my vision. In order to see those desires fulfilled, I needed a plan of action—so I received one. Our church had an outreach once a month to the local nursing home. My plan of action was to join that team once every month. I determined to pray to the Lord before I went in order for the way to be prepared by the Spirit. So I went with the team and visited the aged. As I followed the leading of the Lord and the team overseer, I saw my desires fulfilled. We sang songs, prayed for the aged, visited, and brought gifts. As I engaged in the outreach, I brought comfort and salvation to those in the home. My vision was fulfilled and I changed lives in the nursing home. I was used by God to be a world-changer and a history-maker...at least in that nursing home. I will see many of those elderly people I prayed for in Heaven because of my vision and plan of action. In time, I was assigned to be the leader of the nursing home outreach. My influence expanded as I raised up teams to go into various nursing homes every week.

My nursing home vision and plan of action was a small, simple, and uncomplicated project. I was faithful in the little. Now, I have vision on larger levels. I can carry more weight now because I built up.

Once you have defined your vision, then make a plan of action and follow through. Remember to start small and work those muscles of faith, perseverance, and love.

## Finish Strong

World-changers and history-makers don't give up when the going gets tough. They press through and allow the sufferings, persecutions, and resistance to work as stepping stones instead of stumbling blocks. Jesus endured the cross. When the going got tough, He pressed on through. He finished strong. Paul finished strong. John finished strong. God's world-changers and history-makers finish strong.

If you are in the midst of a battle, remember that glory is right around the corner. Rewards are for the faithful. You can do it. Press on through, and when the going gets tough, remember the other champions who finished strong. You can do it!!

## You Want to Change the World?

Then go for it! What is stopping you? You were made for this very purpose. Let your life count…for Him! Start now. One day at a time. One life at a time.

## Points to Ponder

1. "Talk + Action = Accomplishment." Do you ever find yourself saying any of those statements given at the beginning of this chapter? "One day I am going to..." Take a minute and jot down some ways you might finish that sentence. Now determine a plan of action and "invite the Lord to give you a plan for walking it out."

2. "Greatness comes as a result of one choice at a time, so be intentional with your choices." Think back over your life to see how your past choices have affected your present state, as well as the people around you. What choices are you facing right now?

3. "When you make your list of the things that you are passionate about, you will begin to define vision." Take a moment and make a list of things you're passionate about. Now, "focus on those things and dream on!"

# CHAPTER 3

# It's Time for Change

## D.M. Collins

*I have come to cast fire upon the earth; and how I wish it were already kindled!* (Luke 12:49 NASB)

Everybody seems to agree that the world needs to change, but there is little agreement about what needs to change and how to cause change to happen. Changing the world isn't primarily about laws, economics, politics, and governments. Institutions and structures exist for the benefit of—and too often the manipulation of—people. Every system will operate effectively and with high efficiency when the hearts of the people who run them and are served by them are changed. One thing is certain: hearts cannot be legislated nor controlled in militarized zones. Only lasting change at the heart level will bring unity and true community among all people.

How, then, can hearts be changed in such a way that everyone benefits and none would suffer?

A couple of millennia ago, a young Middle Eastern man caused a transformational change-of-heart to sweep the entire planet. He came with solutions to every problem, forgiveness and freedom for the guilty, and abundant prosperity without end for every man, woman, and child to enjoy throughout all generations. But He didn't do anything on His own. His strategic, unseen Partner guided Him through every challenge and circumstance. This Partner brought supernatural authority and limitless power into the earth through the daily life of a guy who used to run the family business, but one day struck out to fulfill His own destiny.

For three years Jesus and His Partner moved among the people of His homeland: teaching, providing, healing, forgiving, and correcting. Before He died, He passed on His legacy—His unseen Partner—to His best friends. He charged them with doing what He had done and teaching people everywhere to do the same. The concept caught on, and soon after, a sweeping transformation of the entire culture was evident and spreading like wildfire. Somewhere along the way, the wildfire was brought under control and life on planet Earth returned to its former state of widespread oppression and suffering.

How then can we, the rightful heirs to the legacy of Jesus Christ, re-ignite the fire that sets all people free? I believe that we need to start by getting out of "church." After ten years of church-driven life, I firmly believe that "church" ⹂ a place to pass through, not a place to camp for the rest of our lives. Our training manual, the Bible, states over and over that we are to be "in Christ," not "in church." Christ is mobile; "church" is not. Christ is alive; "church" is not.

Jesus left clear instructions to go into the world and announce the arrival of the Kingdom of Heaven on the earth. Those who choose to submit to this supernatural government must first be cleansed and healed from the effects of their former ruler, taught how to live under the reign of the conquering King, and trained in spiritual boot camp to learn the proper care and use of the weaponry that has been assigned for their strategic tasks. Then the newly freed citizens must be mobilized and sent out into the world to spread all the benefits of this good Kingdom to all who would receive it.

This scenario demonstrates the roles of evangelists, pastors, and teachers in the household of God. Only a few will be trained to train others as they process through from darkness into Light. The majority will be sent out as armed-and-ready emissaries of Life into the trenches of every sphere of society and culture: business and research, governance and protection, medicine and education, arts and entertainment, communications and media. All these will know the voice of the Lord. All will lead by serving others' needs and will serve by leading others into solutions for every problem, challenge, and opportunity.

rs in every sphere are those who see and
ges of Heaven's Partner. Some will run ahead
pack, scouting out the movements of those who still
serve the dark kingdom. Others will become the equivalent
of special-ops forces: crossing enemy lines, infiltrating their
camps, advancing the front lines of Light, and demolishing
the fortresses of darkness. Worshiping, prophetic intercessors
will relay what they see and hear back to the commanders.

The commanders are CEOs and CFOs, mayors and gov-
ernors, administrators and peacekeepers who work together
to implement the Partner's creative strategies and deploy
forces of Light wherever darkness attempts to encroach.
This is one way to envision the roles of prophetic and apostolic leaders. Only the ones who train others to do what
they do will stay "in church." They are the few, the humble,
the servant-leaders of the church. The majority will deploy
into the world and bring Heaven's abundance to the people.
All will remain, at all times, "in Christ."

Unfortunately, today God's people are either held hos-
tage in local churches or are outcasts who know there's gotta
be more to real Life than "doing church." Jesus said He was
sent to seek and save "the lost," those who wander around
outside the walls. They belong to Him and know His voice,
but they are not welcome in religious society. They are continually stalked by the wolves of culture, taken down and
devoured because the shepherds—the ones who are charged
to lead and protect them—have rejected and abandoned
them. Jesus charged Peter to "feed My sheep" and "tend My

lambs", to care for the spiritual newborns and nurture them to maturity, and to teach them the ways of their King and lead them into their rightful place and role in the world, among the nations.

We can't keep doing the same thing all year, for years at a time, and for generations without end. Like the Borg in *Star Trek*, the advancing enemy armies identify a tactical advantage, infiltrate our camps, and quickly adapt to our methods. Overwhelming us and assimilating us into the collective of drones, their only purpose is to serve the Borg Queen (religion spirit) and infect everyone in their path with a "sameness virus." Vital parts of the Body are removed and replaced with mechanical implants that do not truly see, feel, hear, or think. They come back to their stations for periodic recharging of their batteries, similar to Sunday services. Then they go back out to assimilate more into their collective.

I believe that the organized and unified church needs to function like Star Fleet Academy (also from *Star Trek*), a point of entry for new recruits who are highly motivated with a sense of purpose and destiny to serve others. Ideally, this should be the attitude of every true follower of Jesus Christ. He tells us to be students of the Kingdom of Heaven and, at the same time, be the strategic sales and marketing team that enters into all the world, demonstrating creative and powerful Kingdom solutions to every problem. Graduates of this supernatural boot camp will sweep the world, not with Bible verse answers, but with biblical principles applied to life on earth wherever people gather to work, play, and rest.

## Points to Ponder

In your personal journal, write down what you hear, see, or sense without judging as you consider the following questions. Review your journal and watch for recurring themes, messages, and people.

1. Do you know your assignment? Ask your Partner—Holy Spirit—to tell you who you are sent to serve, what you are charged to do, and what you need to do to prepare for your mission.

2. What issues or obstacles do you believe are holding you back from identifying and accomplishing your life's purposes? Ask the Lord to bring healing for your wounds and pain, and genuine forgiveness toward others and yourself. Listen and watch for whatever He would say or show you.

3. What do you love to do? In what kind of environment do you feel most alive and motivated? Do you love the outdoors, the classroom, business settings, or creative arts? If you are not currently experiencing that environment, ask your Partner what changes you can make to move toward that place. Take action on at least one point in the next 24 hours, even if it's just doing some research or making a phone call.

4. What might the world around you look like if you were free, empowered, and equipped to bring Heaven's abundance to earth? Ask for dreams and visions to describe

what change you are destined to bring to people in your spheres of influence. Keep a daily journal of your dreams and visions (or daydreams).

5. Have you overcome challenges in life that you can now lead others through? Where have you been? What have you learned? Recall every time that God showed up and led you through. What skills, abilities, and gifts are yours to bring true changes of hearts to others? Offer them up to your God, thank Him for the boot camp lessons, and tell Him how you would like to lead and love others as He has led and loved you.

# CHAPTER 4

# Beyond the Boundaries

## Rob Coscia

*May Christ through your faith [actually] dwell (settle down, abide, make His permanent home) in your hearts! May you be rooted deep in love and founded securely on love, that you may have the power and be strong to apprehend and grasp with all the saints [God's devoted people, the experience of that love] what is the breadth and length and height and depth [of it]; [that you may really come] to know [practically, through experience for yourselves] the love of Christ, which far surpasses mere knowledge [without experience]; that you may be filled [through all your being] unto all the fullness of God [may have the richest measure of the divine Presence, and become a body wholly filled and flooded with God Himself]!* (Ephesians 3:17-19 AMP)

# So You Want to Change the World?

*I want to know God's thoughts; the rest are details.*
—Albert Einstein

Most of us have heard the aphorism "the definition of insanity is doing the same thing over and over, yet expecting a different result." Most credit Albert Einstein with this, while others credit earlier sources, including Benjamin Franklin. You can imagine a storm-soaked Ben holding the smoldering string of what had been his legendary kite, ruminating on insanity. I prefer to think that the credit does belong to Einstein, however.

In the beginning of the 20th century, Einstein was among those pondering the nature of the subatomic, the universe, and everything in between. Those of like mind realized that if they were to understand the nature of something like light, the mathematical tools they would need would require a severe upgrade. Up to that point, a Newtonian framework was used to pretty much define everything. Unless you could measure it, judge it, or calculate its fall to your head while sitting under an apple tree, it wasn't real. Distance, speed, and time were all limited to what was observable to the five senses.

Einstein isn't as important for his theories of relativity as he is for living a life fearlessly determined to see beyond the conspicuous. He saw beyond the boundaries of conventional science into realities that would paint the universe with colors no one had yet experienced. Those world-changing perspectives on everything from photons to wormholes literally made quantum leaps in mathematics and physics, and created new foundations for exploring the infinite. Einstein said, "The most beautiful thing we can experience is the mysterious. It is the source of all true art and all science. He to whom this emotion is a stranger, who can no longer pause to wonder and stand rapt in awe, is as good as dead: his eyes are closed."[1]

The Church needs a similar upgrade. We are in an amazing season of God's glory being revealed in the earth, and we need new foundations from which our eyes are open to the wonders and mysteries of God. We also need eyes to recognize how some of our beliefs about our relationship with God may have limited us, so that we can remove any hindrances to the moving of His Spirit. I've been in many church leadership meetings in which the insanity quote was invoked, but all that changed was a reshuffling of programs, an emphasis on professional performance, and directives to increase the numbers of people in the pews. We need quantum leaps in our intimacy and identity in God, so that we may see ourselves and others as He sees us.

The Church is the Bride, the redeemed Beloved of Jesus Christ, His joy and His only plan for reaching every precious life on this planet. The Church is the family of God, powerful, beautiful, and free. We diminish ourselves when we live below that reality, trading it instead for structures based on fears that corral people into separate conclaves that won't trust each other, much less love each other, in an effort to protect our traditions and positions. We may not do this consciously, but we do it.

Fear that manifests itself when we are living outside of our identity in God is usually rooted in the belief that if we fail God (i.e., the church), we become failure itself, unworthy of love, acceptance, and favor. We convince ourselves that we do not deserve to live in joyful pursuit of an extraordinary life. We place ourselves in isolation, individually or denominationally, trusting no one outside our walls. We live from earth toward Heaven, striving to figure out what God wants of us based on our church's past experiences with Him. Because experience is anathema to the control fear has on us, we live believing healing, miracles, signs, and wonders are evil, or that we are unworthy of them. And there we stay. We spend our spiritual lives hoping an apple drops on our heads as a sign of His approval of what we are doing.

When we base our identity in our own efforts to be acceptable to a seemingly distant God, we will easily judge other people's value based on how they live their lives in relation to the rules of behavior we are struggling with ourselves. In that reality, there is no family of God, only the business of religion. Holiness gets defined by my separateness, not from sin but apart from everything and everyone not acceptable to my fear. Real holiness is a life stewarding my intimacy with the Father, and living out that love in relation to others. Grace is living with a God-consciousness, not a sin-consciousness. This is the Kingdom to which Jesus was inviting people. This is the quantum leap.

In the Bible, Jesus challenged people with questions that would lead them to deeper levels of intimacy with Him. With almost everyone He encountered, He opened a doorway for them from their reality to His. Some went through the door; others didn't. The rich young ruler of Mark 10 had an amazing offer from Jesus to follow Him. The issue wasn't money per se, but the willingness to leave a natural level of trust for a supernatural one. I love that Mark recounts Jesus' love for this young man. Jesus wasn't judging this person for his wealth, but was creating a way for him to come into the fullness of his identity in Christ.

The Emmaus Road disciples, the woman at the well, Zacchaeus, Nathanael, Nicodemus, Peter, John, Matthew, Thomas, Judas—they and everyone else were all challenged by the Living Word to recognize their need for a greater revelation of who they were in Him, and of who they were in relation to themselves and others. *"No longer do I call you servants, for a servant does not know what his master is doing; but I have called you friends, for all things that I heard from My Father I have made known to you"* (John 15:15 NKJV). Jesus was and is inviting those who love Him to see the doorway to even greater intimacy with Him and clearer identity in Him.

Our identity is shaped by the reality we choose to live in. The depths of love, joy, peace, and every other fruit of His Spirit we experience is determined by that reality. That's because we have the power to give meaning to the world around us. I know that sounds like heresy, but it's absolutely true. Jesus said He is *"the Way, the Truth, and the Life"* (see

John 14:6)—but I give meaning to that. I can reject it as a lie, or I can let it penetrate my heart and change me.

*"Behold, I say to you, lift up your eyes and look at the fields, for they are already white for harvest!"* (John 4:35 NKJV). How do you see? Not *what* do you see. We all see the fields. But *how* do you process the vision? Do you see with the eyes of a servant? Being a servant is a powerful part of our life in God, but Jesus invited the disciples to much more. A servant may only see that field in terms of the task. People are simply "the harvest," a goal. A servant's relationship to his master is in the form of orders, not intimacy. If the servant fails, he lives in shame, because there is nowhere else to go. Servants have little relationship with each other and even less freedom.

The upgraded reality of "friend" brings a new perspective. Friends have far greater relationship, and know they are chosen, not hired or indentured. But God doesn't stop there. He invites us to know Him as sons and daughters, as unconditionally loved children. Sons aren't afraid of losing relationship with the King; they are always sons. When they hear a call for battle, they don't see it as a draft in which they have no choice; they see it as expanding the Kingdom of which they are royal inheritors and co-laborers. They see the fields as dearly loved brothers and sisters who are that inheritance, their family in joy and love forever.

World-changers are sons and daughters. They are lovers of God; they know the battle is over intimacy and identity.

They know that whatever we are intimate with, that's what we will produce. They are so secure in the love of the Father that they truly celebrate when someone they have nurtured goes beyond them in authority and influence; they have a passion for recognizing the glory of God in others, and a desire for equipping them to live in that glory.

World-changers know that to actually bring change to the earth, they have to recognize and embrace the transitions that God desires in them and their generation. If Jesus invites them to eat His flesh and drink His blood, though they may not fully understand it, they know it's an invitation to life, a leap into the beautiful mysterious. World-changers know how to see.

## Points to Ponder

1. Find a quiet spot and allow your heart to be at rest. Let Holy Spirit really permeate you with His peace. He is for you, not against you. You are His child, and He delights to bless you. Be patient; bask in His love. When you feel you are at peace, then ask God who you are. Everyone's different—you may see a picture, hear a word audibly, or the words may just pop into your heart. What is He saying about you? Then write down what you've heard without overanalyzing it.

2. When He has shown you how amazing He thinks you really are, then trust Him to reveal what areas there may be in your life that are blocking you from living daily in the reality He just showed you.

3. Take one of those issues that He has identified as a constraint or limiting belief in your life (assuming you have any) and ask Him where it is coming from, where it's rooted. Ask Him to show you how to address it. Is forgiveness needed? Is a new perspective in order? He specializes in quantum leaps; trust Him to tell you where to make that leap.

4. When you are done, ask Him to show you your family and friends. How does He see them? What are they created for? When He tells you, don't try and make them into what you see, just bless them and encourage them with what you see in them. Let your peace permeate

every place you go, so that others experience freedom when you are around. This is living as a world-changer.

*We are slaves when we live in the reality of what others say about us. We are task masters when we tell others how they should live. We are free when we live in the reality of who God says we are. We are liberators when we celebrate the freedom of others.*

## Endnote

1. http://www.heartquotes.net/Einstein.html; accessed October 11, 2010.

# CHAPTER 5

# Change Begins Within

## Barbie Breathitt

*Now after John had been taken into custody, Jesus came into Galilee, preaching the gospel of God, and saying, "The time is fulfilled, and the kingdom of God is at hand; repent and believe in the gospel"* (Mark 1:14-15 NASB).

If you truly love, you can change the world. God so loved the cosmos that He sent Jesus, His only son, to save the world from sin and darkness. Jesus came not as a ruling king but as a servant, the son of a poor carpenter. Although He was a son of a blue collar worker, He was also the son of God; yet like us He learned obedience through the things He suffered. Jesus discovered that the trials and challenges of life caused Him to seek both His earthly and heavenly fathers for wisdom, counsel, and advice.

Jesus learned to take pieces of wood to sculpt and chisel them into something functional. Jesus came as a humble servant, yet He was the King of kings, and Creator of the universe. His coming was not in the style, fashion, or manner that any expected. The world He created had no room for His birth.

Man does not need a life of ease or comfort without the tension of conflict because man's growth comes through his struggles to reach higher goals that are worth fighting to obtain. Jesus came to change the world through giving His life. No one is perfect, but through God's perfect love we can love the vilest of enemies until they are transformed into a lover of God and man.

Jesus chose 12 men to disciple. He poured His love, wisdom, and spiritual understanding into them. These men would help usher in a new world order, the Kingdom of God. This is an invisible Kingdom, one that is not limited by space, time, or physical boundaries. The Kingdom is only limited by doubt and unbelief. Doubt is a learned behavior that springs from expectations and hopes that have been dashed. Doubt is one of the great disablers that tries to cripple our faith. We must remove doubt from our paradigm and suspend disbelief. God's Kingdom functions to the measure you can believe and walk in faith. Jesus said, *"Repent,"* that is, "change your mind," *"for the kingdom of heaven is at hand"* (Matt. 3:2 NASB). The people who will change the world are those who preach the pure powerful Gospel of the Kingdom.

Jesus is the master builder. He is the Carpenter who knows how to use every tool of relationship, religion, science, and education to skillfully craft us. Each one of these instruments gives us a particular perspective on life that portrays a limited view of reality. Separately, they bring about an incomplete image or a particular opinion based on man's limited knowledge, his belief structures, or a form of godliness that is void of God's transforming power.

We are the raw blocks of wood. Because we are raw, we need to be ready, able, and willing to change; to be transformed into what Jesus desires and has designed for us. The Holy Spirit is able to use every experience to cut, press, hammer, and fashion us into something beautiful. When we love God, every detail in our lives will be worked into something good, enabling us to reach our greatest potential. Pay close attention to the truth that is in Christ that enables us to do away with our old life of sinful ignorance.

Take for instance our desire to see the world changed or influenced by our life. If there is no difference in our lifestyle, what do we really have to offer the people who live without God? If our relationship with God is so tenuous that we are not overcoming, or we don't have a better (more joyful) approach to the dilemmas that face us each day, then why would an unbeliever even notice us and attempt to follow our example? We must be offering an example to be noticed if we ever expect the world to be influenced by our life and experiences.

It is a wonderful experience when we reach the point of salvation. We recognize who Jesus is and what He accomplished on the cross. There He made restitution between man and God. The sin that separated us from God is now removed and in God's sight we are again accepted as His children and part of His living, vibrant family (as it was in the Garden). But if we remain in the fallen world of sin and debauchery, then how has our experience of salvation really helped our witness? We must press on and into the deeper things of life, leaving behind all the encumbrances that weigh us down and keep our relationship with God sullied and stale.

Once we let go of these petty strings that bind us to the world and its fake shiny allure, we are better able to step into the realm of spiritual living. We will focus more of our time on God and allow His love to change us, not only in the thought realm but also in the realm of experience. We will believe God and expect Him to move on our behalf when we pray. We have confidence to ask God to step in and give His guidance when making decisions.

Ask Him to intervene when cuts at the factory are expected. Ask God to open the door to a new job if you get cut from the factory. Have confidence that if the very world should shake and fall from under your feet that your faith is not going to be shaken. When the world sees this kind of confidence, they will take notice.

As God works His character and conduct in us by renewing the spirit of our minds from the inside out, we can live a life fashioned by the Master. God comes to take the chaos and void places of darkness out of our life and replace them with His peace that passes all of our ability to understand. If we want to be world-changers, these changes must first start with each one of us totally surrendering to the skillful hand of the master builder. He who has begun a good work in us is faithful to finish that work and create a masterpiece from a raw piece of wood.

We must see ourselves as only beginning the journey of transformation and not having arrived. Now is the best time to change because now is the only time we have, and it is only a fleeting moment. We have been given great power and authority to change and mold our world, to remove things that harm and limit this generation by changing the way we think and respond to situations.

Our attitude is only one aspect of our relationship with God that should be changed with the realization of our salvation. One of the other areas of our faith walk should include miracles. This is a supernatural way to change man's belief systems. To show God actually intervening in the world of natural causes and effects is a powerful way to bring people to a point of decision. Will men acknowledge that healing takes place or will their "world view," which denies the intervention of God, stop them from believing? Many people believe, like the deists, that there may be a God who made the world but He does not interfere with the events of the world. They believe we live in a closed system where only natural things occur. They would conclude that earthquakes are only natural events where the tectonic plates rub against each other and shift suddenly. Snowfalls that are unprecedented are only because the warming of the earth is throwing the balance of seasons off. They would say that all the changes taking place on the earth may be explained away and left at the feet of natural causes.

For believers this is not acceptable. We know it is God who brings the rain or who withholds His blessing. When Elijah prayed, it did not rain for three years on the face of the earth. Was this a coincidence, a natural cause, and did Elijah simply "time" his prayer well like the cadence of a well-timed "rain dance"? Or did God actually intervene and hold back the clouds and rain in answer to Elijah's prayer? As Christians we believe it was God who moved into the natural realm and held back the rain. We are in a battle of beliefs.

Jesus changed the world by changing the lives of 12 men. He gave them the revelation of His perfect love and restored them to a place of intimacy. In that place they were given a new identity as sons. Their sonship released them into their destiny as world-changers. These 12 men turned the then-known world right side up as they advanced the Kingdom of God.

We, as Kingdom builders, are in a battle. It is a battle to not only influence but also to overcome the world. Jesus told us His Kingdom would never be erased but it would continue to grow and expand and cover the whole world. This is not a physical battle, in that we pick up arms and start shooting the infidel, but it is a spiritual battle fought on our knees in prayer with love and compassion.

It is a physical battle in the sense that we have to constantly be on guard against allowing this world, our physical bodies, and evil influences from dragging us down and causing us to stumble back into our former ways. We do fight physically by fasting and praying and spending time with other wiser and more adept believers. We do fight physically because to stop breathing is to stop fighting in the physical realm. You are still breathing, aren't you? Then you are in the flesh.

When we take the time to fast and pray, we are guaranteed that our prayers are heard. The fasting helps us reach the spiritual point where we are confident God will empower us to meet the next battle or challenge. If you are not fasting, then you may find that you are just a little apprehensive as to the outcome of your prayers or to the next challenge against the world and your flesh.

Believers are called to pour Christ and His grace into the people they meet, equipping them to advance to the next level of discipleship. We should treat everyone we meet with respect and honor as if they have already received Christ. We are prone to immense evil and enormous good in the same life. Walking in love's compassion and striving to forgive others is our only saving grace. If we forgive, we will be forgiven and a great change will take place in us and in others. The goal is to change people one at a time, and then send them out to change the ones they can influence. This exponentially increases the Kingdom of God as it is built around the person of Jesus Christ. Carriers of God's presence change the world; without His presence we become part of the problem instead of being the answer.

We are called to be prophets like Elijah. Indeed Moses wished that all would prophesy; but instead of climbing the mountain to enter the presence of God with the prophet Moses, the people cowered at the base of the flaming, quaking mountain and told Moses to go in their place. They knew that if they did not change, the presence of God's fire would consume them. God is once again calling us all to be the prophet, to stand in the place of Moses, and have a face-to-face encounter with God. We are once again called to climb the mountain and call out in God's presence for Him to intervene into the natural realm of our lives and those of our neighbors. We are called to intervene in areas of the world where "natural" disasters or God's mighty hand is displayed.

The whole earth is now groaning in anticipation of the appearance of the sons of God. The earth is shaking and quaking and reeling about with changes in atmosphere on every front. We are called to step forward in the power of God to speak peace to and calm the storms of life. The sons of God are at the point of being manifest to the world as world-changers who have the power to affect the natural realm with the supernatural hand of God. Pray against the evil effects of the hurricane's destructive wind. Pray against the ground opening up and swallowing whole cities. Ask God to intervene on your neighbor's behalf and when drought and famine cleave to the empty stomachs of emaciated children. Bring the healing compassion of Jesus to sway and call the fallen cosmos to be redeemed.

We must not be caught up in the argument of whose sin caused the tower to fall. It is not for us to decide. What we are to look for is how the battle will be won. Will we react with the love and compassion of Jesus and extend a helping hand? We can offer physical aid in the form of money, time, food, and even blankets to those who are disadvantaged or suffering from the wreckage of a fallen world. We are called to do this and more. We are called to be like Elijah and pray that the rain of God's Spirit will return. We are called to show God's hand even more powerfully than the terrors of night and day to heal and restore.

Aaron saw the hand of God moving to strike rebellious Israel, but he was not static and contemplative. Aaron ran to the altar and grabbed burning coals and ran in front of the oncoming slaughter. Aaron, as the priest he was called to be, stood in intercession between the wrath of God and the world, and God answered his faith. God was moved to stop the slaughter. We are called to be priests to the world.

I'm not suggesting we all go to Haiti and hand out blankets, unless you feel this call from God. What I am challenging you to do is realize that you can be in Haiti as you stand on your knees before a gracious and merciful God and cry out for salvations, healing, and for the heart of all around you to be changed and restored.

In the sphere of man's education no one would attend a university if the school kept charging for more courses but never scheduled a graduation where degrees were awarded when earned. This is in contrast to the example of Jesus who constantly sent His disciples out to learn through experience but didn't revoke their ordination when they failed. He lovingly corrected, advised, and released more disciples.

When we walk in the light Jesus supplies, having the eyes of our heart enlightened by His love, receiving His truth is not difficult. The difficulty comes in remaining humble and teachable. We must remember that we are the students and Jesus is the teacher and the plumb line by which we measure our lives. The apostle Paul said, "I have not arrived. I don't have it all together. I strive toward the goal and reach out to Christ who first reached out to me. I am not an expert but I have my eyes on the high call and the goal and I am moving forward. I am not turning back. I am totally committed. I want everything God has for me; my eyes are focused on Him alone" (see Phil. 3:11-14).

We, like Paul, are headed upward, in the right direction. It is important to stay focused, on track, and to keep running the race with those who are on the same course and have the same goal. There are many paths and goals to choose from in life, but if it's not a God path, it will lead to a dead end. There is only one way that leads to eternal life, and that is through the cross of Jesus to God. Pick up your cross, take the first step, forge a path to travel, then others will follow on the road you make. Walk with a friend and you will have fellowship. Assist an enemy and you will change the world.

Paul said, "Follow me as I follow Christ" (see 1 Cor. 11:1 AMP). To follow Christ takes courage.

Courage enables one to release the secure places of the familiar to embrace the adventure of the fresh unknown. Christ's path leads down avenues of the unknown where we will meet new people and experience strange and exciting events. To remain static and fearful while holding onto the familiar will hinder our walk into the miraculous Kingdom of God. There is no value in holding onto the old if it doesn't bring forth the power to change and renew one's life.

It was the saints who stood in the Roman arenas and faced hungry lions and did not waver in their resolve to follow Jesus as the one and only God. Their heroic stand caused the numbers in their ranks who called themselves "Christians" to swell. How are you responding to the crises going on all around you? Do the earthquakes, or hurricanes, or the rumors of war shake your faith in God? Do others see you quivering in your boots at the terrors coming on the earth or are you steadfast in your faith, unwavering in your devotion, and brave enough to hold to the name of Jesus in the face of ridicule and malice?

Change is timeless, everlasting, and unending. Change has many apprentices but no experts. Experts in any field are highly valued and admired in our society. However, even in their success, many experts are generally afraid to take risks or explore a range of new possibilities. The goal of most students or beginners is to mimic their mentor, removing ignorance and obtaining greater knowledge, skill, and information. Students know that if they keep doing what they cannot do well, they will finally master it and reach the status of an expert, obtaining their goal. The teacher's goal is to have his students excel above and beyond his abilities. Jesus said, "Greater works shall you do."

What is the proper way to relate to knowledge and the use of information? Does knowledge cause us to broaden our scope of inquiry? Does the knowledge we gain cause us to question how, when, or why? Do we settle for status quo or shoot for the impossible? Learning is more than knowing details, information, and facts. Knowledge is not intelligence, but it leads to truth. Revelation of truth without a manifestation of that truth in our lives only remains information. If we never explore the unknown or solve the unsolvable, we will remain on a neutral plain of dissatisfaction. If we teach the Kingdom from a relational standpoint, people will be faithful, flourish, and grow. If we constantly point toward the goal (which is Christ) and the avenue to gain the goal (which is to build the Kingdom of God), then we have a timeless, everlasting, never-ending goal. So, we are ever learning and ever changing while being transformed into the image of Christ.

God gives us wisdom and revelation in the knowledge of Christ. He opens the eyes of our hearts with spiritual enlightenment so we can understand the great hope He has given us as we believe Him. As we believe God, our inner man is strengthened by increased faith and a greater measure of love for mankind, and our knowledge of Christ expands. The more we know Christ the more His love floods us until we overflow with the fullness of His power. When we know Him we are able to do great exploits to impact generation after generation. If we don't know Christ and the power of His love to change us, we remain powerless, and cannot change ourselves or the world around us.

In a child's mind there are many possibilities; in the adult's mind, there are few. A child sees things the way they are, not the way they must be; therefore we must analyze life with an open, childlike mind…change your mind, repent, and hope eternal will spring up. A child's faith is pure, simple, and teachable so children easily enter the Kingdom. We know who we are; what we need to discover is who we can become in God. It is easier to teach children something they have never known than it is to reeducate people who think they already know something. Believers in the Body of Christ must pursue the knowledge of the mystery contained in Christ.

Walking in a new direction or starting over is difficult if we feel we have already journeyed miles down the road but in the wrong direction. A new direction means change, and change is difficult. It requires a lot of energy to stop the progress down a particular path only to reverse course and retrace the steps back to where we started. There are occasions when God's plan is not followed and His directions are ignored. In these situations God will often bring the necessary pain and abrasion in order to bring enough discomfort to our lives that we will want to change course, if for no other reason then to stop the pain. Once the course correction has taken place and we are back on the prescribed path God originally proposed, the pain ceases and we realize we are back on course.

Progress means carrying success into your future while leaving failures far behind. Wisdom enables you to discover the knowledge of how you got off the path, but leave the hurt and disappointment in the past. Overcoming disappointment and becoming a success is as easy as implementing Plan B. The past hurts are left to die and fade from the conscious mind.

Significant change seldom comes by accident but more by design, and when it does come it leaves a monument that beckons us to remember who we were and evaluate who we want to become by making strategic choices for a lifetime. Changing the world begins one moment in time. Now is the time to change the world.

Change should cause both positive and constructive forward movement—even if it causes questions, conflict, and friction. We will progress through life successfully if we don't become stagnant and stationary, droning on about past failures and dwelling on our shortcomings, but continue to grow and change. We must not look to change simply to have change. Our progress must be in the prescribed path and direction ordained by God. We need to follow God's path of truth, not just any path we would choose that leads to change for change's sake.

Isaiah instructs us to behold or see that God is doing a new thing (see Isa. 43:19). Tradition is the greatest hindrance to a move of God in our lives. When God wants to reveal or speak something new to us, we relate to the new by the old things of our previous experiences. If we continue to maintain what we are, we will never know who we can become. God has to plow our fallow ground so we can hear Him in a new way. He comes to declare change, but we are scared to calculate how the impact of these changes will affect our life. We want to know the outcome so we can decide if we want to follow the prescribed path. If the prescribed path seems to contradict our current level of knowledge and our tradition, we have added another hindrance to our will to obey. We unwittingly become the judge of God's plan instead of a follower. We elevate ourselves to the level of God, and without the complete knowledge that God has, we make our own choices and decisions.

Not only do we put ourselves in the place to judge our own lives, but we also point the finger at others' actions and wrongly judge according to our limited knowledge. God is fully capable of directing people in their own particular paths that He has chosen for them; this will cause them to reach their prescribed destiny. So we are not to judge now because we do not have all the information. When the light of the Lord comes to expose every hidden thing of darkness and He also reveals the secrets and purposes of the heart, His righteous judgment will come.

Changes do not come without a fight, a conversion, or killing of the old ways of thinking, or recognizing our defaults and habits. If we want someone or something to be different, the surest way to receive that desire is to be different ourselves. We need to have our minds renewed, so that we can relay it in a new way instead of in the old pattern. Nothing in God is old; all things in Him are bright always and consistent with no shadows. God is not only yesterday, He is present, future, omnipotent, strong, and powerful; He is the Alpha and the Omega. We cannot stay the same as we behold Him—we change from glory to glory as we are confronted with God. We can't come to God in ignorance without being changed.

God challenges us to continue seeking Him when we don't receive the needed answers. We cannot depend on our reasoning or limited intelligence. Proverbs tells us to acknowledge Him in all our ways and He will direct our path. We must come to a place where we cannot lean on our own understanding so God has to bring our limited understanding to an end. He wants to take us to a higher reality.

Life is formed by a series of choices and beliefs that are followed; to change, you only need to repent, change your mind, and realign your priorities. Life is full of changes in all dimensions: past, present, and future. To forget one dimension is to be locked in time with no hope for tomorrow. To live means change and the hope of self-renewal, to change is to advance, to advance is to continue maturing and transforming into someone who is full of godly wisdom.

## Points to Ponder

1. What are some of the main points from this chapter? Take a moment to look back over the preceding pages and list them.

2. "If we want to be world-changers, these changes must first start with each one of us totally surrendering to the skillful hand of the master builder." Are you willing to change? Are you ready to put yourself into the hands of God so He can mold, chisel, and shape you any way He wants?

3. Do you feel challenged about something specific in your life? Write it down and talk to God about it.

CHAPTER 6

# *You Can Be a World-Changer*

## Adam LiVecchi

*I can do all things through Christ which strengtheneth me* (Philippians 4:13 KJV).

Real and long-lasting change starts on the inside. Real Christianity can be defined in one verse, Galatians 1:16, which says: *"To reveal His Son in me, that I might preach Him among the heathen; immediately I conferred not with flesh and blood"* (KJV). Christianity is having a revelation of Jesus Christ and giving it away. Also, Christianity is not being under the control of men, but being under the shadow of His wings. There is no real Christianity without the Secret Place. The Secret Place is not only praying with the door closed, although it certainly begins there. The Secret Place is a life hidden in Christ. When the Lord told Samuel to anoint David, he did. David said in Psalm 23 (NKJV), *"You anoint my head with oil.*" He was referring to the Lord Jesus, his Shepherd. However, if you read the account of him being anointed in the Book of Samuel, you will see that Samuel anointed him. One day I was reading Psalm 23 and Jesus spoke to me and said, "I never anointed him; Samuel did. But when Samuel obeyed My word, he became invisible and David saw Me." Real ministry is when people see Jesus through our obedience to His word.

When lions couldn't eat Daniel, it was because he was under the shadow of His wings in the Secret Place. Tradition says that John the Revelator was thrown in boiling oil to be burned alive, twice. The oil could not burn his physical body because he was in the Secret Place. A crowd of people wanted to grab Jesus and throw Him off a mountain, yet He managed to walk through the crowd untouched—He was abiding in the Secret Place. Paul was hidden away for three years, and then he went into one of the most powerful apostolic ministries the world has ever seen.

When the veil of Jesus' flesh was torn, we were all invited to live in the Secret Place forever. There is no greater honor than to live from God's presence toward the circumstances of our daily lives, as well as the problems the earth is facing. Anything sustainable will require change; the only exception is Jesus Christ who is the same yesterday, today, and forever.

Change is very uncomfortable to most people because we have to give up control. When Peter and the other men left everything, they were saying that a change in their life was absolutely necessary. They were willing to give up control. If we are not willing to give up control, we are not willing to follow Jesus.

Life is filled with choices; the average person makes roughly 300 choices per day. However, the person in prison makes roughly 10 choices per day. If we make bad choices, our ability to influence others for good becomes vastly reduced and our God-given potential is no longer attainable. The Good News is that the Gospel of Jesus Christ is for both the prisoner and the captive according to Isaiah 61:1 (KJV):*"The Spirit of the LORD God is upon Me; because the LORD hath anointed Me to preach good tidings unto the meek; He hath sent Me to bind up the brokenhearted, to proclaim liberty to the captives, and the opening of the prison to them that are bound."* The prisoner is the man or woman who broke the law and so legally deserves prison. The captive is someone who was captured in the battle. Whether you are a captive of religion or a prisoner of sin, Jesus Christ says "freedom" to you! That is good news.

The good news is for everyone, yet not everyone will receive it. However, I am sure you will! God trusts you; He has entrusted the Gospel of the Kingdom to you. An insecure leader or pastor who has been bitten by the sheep may not trust you, but an all-knowing God has entrusted you with Himself. Therefore, according to Heaven you are trustworthy, and God desires you to know Him and be used of Him.

Most of the world has a negative view of Christians because people who don't really know Jesus have deeply misrepresented Him. However, we have the privilege to represent who He really is to the world. My prayer before I minister is simply, "Holy Spirit, put Jesus on display." That is what the world needs. They don't need an introduction to a two-day-a-week religious organization that wants their time and money and gives them nothing in return.

I love church and I love gathering together to pursue the throne of grace, but what I don't enjoy is when, as soon as we get to the throne of grace, it becomes time to come back down to reality for announcements. When our agenda is more important than God's presence, we have become idolaters in the deepest way. A seared conscience can't discern God's presence or hear His voice. We must return to our first love and He will cleanse our conscience.

We as a people have to become more sensitive to God's presence. When we are not sensitive to God's presence, it just reveals that our hearts are hard and self-centered and self-willed and we have not given Jesus control. A real Christian's greatest desire is the manifest presence of the Lord, where He speaks from the most Holy Place.

Jesus taught us how to pray, and it was simple: *"...on earth as it is in heaven"* (Luke 11:2 AMP). Heaven is filled and even lit by the manifest presence of God. The heavenly city is illuminated by light that shines forth from a wounded Lamb. Our life must be filled with that same light. If our lives are not, then we need a new strategy, called the "Ancient Paths." The Ancient Paths are simply doing things God's way simply because He said so. The Ancient Paths are from and to the Secret Place. Jeremiah and Isaiah were commissioned from the Secret Place. Calling is established, and we are commissioned and sent from God's presence to speak His Word and do His work. That is real faith that pleases God. Real faith is attained as God speaks.

The Ancient Paths are us walking in what God has said and is saying. They are the unchanging truths that God through His Holy Spirit has predestined us to walk in and experience that we may be conformed into the image of Christ Jesus. Christ is formed in us as He speaks to us and we obey Him. When we choose to please God, everyone around us may not be happy, but that is not so important anyway. We learn from one of Jesus' sermons that He wasn't very *seeker friendly*—especially when He said in John 6:53 (KJV): *"Then Jesus said unto them, Verily, verily, I say unto you, Except ye eat the flesh of the Son of man, and drink His blood, ye have no life in you."* I guess He wasn't too worried about what the crowd thought or felt?

Maybe Jesus was more interested in pleasing His Father than men. The good news is that Jesus is fully committed to making us like Him. The way God conforms us is in His presence and by His word and as we are led by His Holy Spirit.

*We can change the world around us because He has changed the world in us.* We have been given an unshakeable Kingdom.

I learned a lot about the unshakeable Kingdom being in the epicenter of the earthquake in Haiti on January 12, 2010. When the earth shook, the Church did not. The reason it didn't shake is because it was a Church built on the Kingdom and the Kingdom does not shake. However, there are three things that are necessary if we are going to change the world. We must be people of His Presence. In the Old Testament there was no way into the Holy of Holies. There was no door or entrance or slit in the huge curtain called the "veil" that separated the Holy Place from the Most Holy Place. If God did not supernaturally draw or transport the priest into the Holy of Holies, he could not get there. That is why Jesus said in John 6:44 (KJV), *"No man can come to Me, except the Father which hath sent Me draw him: and I will raise him up at the last day."* The priest could not get through the veil; in the same way we cannot come to Jesus without the Father drawing us. We must become a crucified people who are not self-willed, so that we can be moved by God and not by what we want.

*The second thing* that is necessary for us to be world-changers is we must obey the Word of God and walk by faith and not by sight. Paul said we walk by faith and not by sight. I think Peter walking on the water to Jesus on the sea is the best and most clear picture of that verse. God wants us to not only hear the word of the Lord but to see it also, as He said to Jeremiah, "see the word of the Lord." When Peter was walking by *faith*, he was walking; when he started to walk by *sight*, he immediately began to sink. We must be people who choose to step out of the boat and walk by faith with Jesus.

Before the disciples knew it was Jesus they were frightened, so then Peter steps in. Matthew 14:27-29 (KJV) says,

> *But straightway Jesus spake unto them, saying, Be of good cheer; it is I; be not afraid. And Peter answered Him and said, Lord, if it be Thou, bid me come unto Thee on the water. And He said, Come. And when Peter was come down out of the ship, he walked on the water, to go to Jesus.*

Peter was the one who responded to God; Jesus was talking to everyone yet only Peter answered God.

Also, when Jesus said to Peter, "Come," He didn't say, "Peter come." He said, "Come." All 12 of the disciples could have come, but only Peter did. The man who has ears to hear is the man who will step out. Eleven men had a story, while only one man had a testimony. Eleven men had a doctrine about the power of God, and one man had an experience with it. We must choose to step out of the boat in this hour. I believe God is looking for a company of people to step out of the boat. Will you be that person? Will we be that people?

*The third thing* that is necessary to be a world-changer is to heed Jesus' last words that He said on earth. The last thing He said is probably very important. Acts 1:8 (KJV) says,

*But ye shall receive power, after the Holy Ghost is come upon you: and ye shall be witnesses unto Me both in Jerusalem, and in all Judea, and in Samaria, and unto the uttermost part of the earth.*

In Matthew 24 you have two kinds of people. Those who are deceived, who are offended, who betray each other, whose love grows cold, and who are not ready for the Lord Jesus' appearance or His return. Then you have those who are faithful, who are persecuted, and who endure. The latter are the people I believe you are—those who will heed Jesus' last words on earth and take the Gospel of the Kingdom to the nations. We have freely received Jesus and we must be willing to give Him away. If we want to start a war on terror, then we should preach the Love of Jesus Christ to a hungry Muslim soul. We must choose to be a people who obey the One we call Lord. We must preach the Gospel of the Kingdom to the nations and also to those who are right in front of us.

A fresh release of missionaries filled with love and power will be completely necessary if we are going to see Jesus' prayer answered *"on earth as it is in heaven."* Let me reassure you, His prayer will be answered. Revelation 11:15 (KJV) says,

*And the seventh angel sounded; and there were great voices in heaven, saying, The kingdoms of this world are become the kingdoms of our Lord, and of His Christ; and He shall reign forever and ever.*

## Points to Ponder

1. What can you do to further honor Jesus in the sphere of influence God has already given you?

2. As you spend time with Jesus, what are some practical things you can do to set yourself apart from distractions?

3. As you move from the Secret Place to the marketplace or just back to plain life, how can you obey what He is saying and step out in faith today?

# CHAPTER 7

# Spiritual Unity

## Abby Abildness

*And the glory which You gave Me [Jesus], I have given them, that they may be one just as We are one…and that the world may know that You have sent Me, and have loved them as You have loved Me* (John 17:22-23 NKJV).

Jesus' last heart cry was that we would be "one" that the world would see! He longed for a spiritual unity of all believers that would be manifested in the life of His believing Church Body. He longed that we would bear witness to His divine mission of redeeming people to Himself and His Kingdom of Heaven. The prophet Jeremiah spoke the word of the Lord, saying to the remnant of Israel, *"I will be the God of all the families [tribes] of Israel, and they shall be My people...I have loved you with an everlasting love; therefore I have drawn you with lovingkindness"* (Jer. 31:1,3 NASB).

In my Healing Tree International missions to the Middle East I found myself in deep spiritual conversation with a fervent Sunni Sheikh. We agreed that Jesus was a great prophet and teacher, and the conversation escalated to a climax with me saying He is "King over all Kings." The sheikh said he would rule even higher as king above every king. I agreed until he said, "World Domination by Jesus Christ." Then I was jolted into the reality that he looked for God as a controlling world dominator, and I was looking for His loving peaceable dominion over all the earth!

## Call to Spiritual Unity

Jesus' "Call to Spiritual Unity" is a call to oneness dependent on seeking the *true* Father's will and being in covenant with Him so we move with what moves His heart. He desires that we would experience His love and bring His love to others that they would join His body of believers. We are in a season of crossing denominational lines and cultural borders into a massive move of God gathering His Bride, building prayer networks, and filling stadiums with global healing ministries, worship concerts, and regional transformation networks wanting to bring His true believers together *as one!*

It is His manifest presence and glory that draws us beyond our borders to minister His Kingdom. Somehow in His presence our religions, denominations, and differing theologies don't seem to be the most important, but rather our central love for Jesus and His love for us transcends our differences. Was Jesus' last prayer a cry for the Church to be one? Did Jesus intend us to separate ourselves into religions and denominations? Did He intend that church would be everyone sitting silently and listening to a speech? Or did He intend people to be consumed by His love that draws all believers to Himself? Did He intend that we convert people to our way of thinking, or did He intend that we exude a love of Christ so compelling that they want to know the God we love?

In our church organizations have we lost heart of this central first love He called for in the messages to the seven churches of Revelation? With all our programming and media did we lose sight of life with the central passion of loving and worshiping the true God and sharing His love that draws us all together? How did we lose focus of beholding Him as our beloved Bridegroom in the garden and how do we restore healing that rescues and revives people back to His loving Kingdom? Did He intend us to convert people to our religious doctrines, or submit to His righteous reign and become living stones building a tower of loving refuge for all to run into?

The world is at a historic juncture in the battle over who will reign over the earth. The battle is ultimately over the truth of who Jesus was and will become. He told the Jews, *"...you shall know the truth, and the truth shall make you free"* (John 8:32 NKJV). All men have a God-shaped vacuum they seek to fill in a myriad of ways, but to many He still is an unknown God. The character and works of God must be seen through us if we are truly His. Jesus said to the Jews, *"If God were your Father, you would love Me, for I proceeded forth...from God"* (John 8:42 NASB). We need to disentangle from compromises that brought God's judgment upon His chosen people. When Elijah went against the prophets of Baal, he was demonstrating the true God to people who were confused about who God really was.

## His Glory Draws Us

If we represent Him well on earth, we will draw men to Him and be manifesting the glory of His Kingdom on earth. On a trip through Turkey into Northern Iraq, I crossed the Chebar Canal where Ezekiel once sat among the exiles seeing a vision of God's glory chariot, where the "wheels within the wheels" traveled together filled with eyes moving across the earth to and fro from one direction to another. I was surprised to see birds flying in circles as though they were the eyes of the wheels within the wheels watching over the people of the earth. Our prayers and alignment with God seemed very close as we sensed we could touch His heart and draw down His power and might. We invited His righteous reign over the earth, and His royal scepter of righteousness to reign over all the earth.

Even sitting in the Middle East where the exiles traveled, I was reminded of the words of "The Battle Hymn of the Republic," penned during the Civil War, during a pivotal moment preserving unity and righteousness.

## "His Truth Is Marching On"

"The Battle Hymn of the Republic" written by Julia Ward Howe still carries our marching orders as His Truth is marching on, bringing His righteous reign to us across the earth:

> Mine eyes have seen the glory of the coming of the
> Lord;
> He is trampling out the vintage where the grapes of
> wrath are stored;
> He hath loosed the fateful lightning of His terrible
> swift sword;
> His truth is marching on.
> Glory! Glory! Hallelujah!
> Glory! Glory! Hallelujah!
> Glory! Glory! Hallelujah!
> His truth is marching on.
>
> I have seen Him in the watch fires of a hundred cir-
> cling camps;
> They have builded Him an altar in the evening
> dews and damps;

I can read His righteous sentence by the dim and
flaring lamps;
His day is marching on.
Glory! Glory! Hallelujah!
Glory! Glory! Hallelujah!
Glory! Glory! Hallelujah!
His day is marching on.

I have read a fiery Gospel writ in burnished rows of
steel;
"As ye deal with My contemners, so with you My
grace shall deal";
Let the Hero, born of woman, crush the serpent
with His heel,
Since God is marching on.
Glory! Glory! Hallelujah!
Glory! Glory! Hallelujah!
Glory! Glory! Hallelujah!
Since God is marching on.

He has sounded forth the trumpet that shall never
call retreat;
He is sifting out the hearts of men before His judg-
ment seat;
Oh, be swift, my soul, to answer Him!
Be jubilant, my feet;
Our God is marching on.
Glory! Glory! Hallelujah!
Glory! Glory! Hallelujah!
Glory! Glory! Hallelujah!
Our God is marching on.

In the beauty of the lilies Christ was born across the
sea,
With a glory in His bosom that transfigures you
and me:
As He died to make men holy, let us live to make
men free;
[*originally*...let us *die* to make men free]
While God is marching on.
Glory! Glory! Hallelujah!
Glory! Glory! Hallelujah!
Glory! Glory! Hallelujah!
While God is marching on.

He is coming like the glory of the morning on the
wave,
He is wisdom to the mighty, He is honor to the
brave;
So the world shall be His footstool, and the soul of
wrong His slave,
Our God is marching on.
Glory! Glory! Hallelujah!
Glory! Glory! Hallelujah!
Glory! Glory! Hallelujah!
Our God is marching on.

We need to rebuild the watch fires of circling camps
of God's people restoring the relational fabric of men and
women being spiritually empowered in our homes and com-
munities throughout the earth. Let men and women not sit
passively in churches but rise up to lead in their families and

circles of influence to be persons of substance and stature; and to cross borders to share the authentic practical expression of our spirituality community by community, family by family, that draws men to the true God.

## We Carry Jesus' Light to the World

Jesus walked in the midst of the lamp stands in the vision of the churches of Revelation, whose congregations still meet in Turkey, and are representative of churches around the world. Jesus still checks our condition, just as the priests trimmed the wick morning and evening to maintain a bright and clear flame. We have a clarion call to be a bright living witness throughout the earth. He will check our condition individually and corporately as He is calling us to move out in our spheres of influence throughout the world while always being connected with Him as His Body of believers.

God is awakening revelation of the coming day of glory and love for the whole earth! He is awakening the Church with His love that we can truly be a lighthouse to wayfarers in the nations. We are becoming a place of refuge and rest, a place to come in to experience the everlasting love of God's family. The power of love is the power that draws people to Him. We have a little historic country church nearby with a message out front that says, "Jesus is Inside. Come and See." He beckons us in to experience the life-changing presence and power of His love. He is the Ancient of Days drawing us from the depths of His love, fulfilling His covenants of generations past. Dig deep and drink deep for the Deep of God calls unto the deep in our hearts!

This happens on a global scale as nations are impacted when their leaders are impacted. Spiritual wells of revival open up wellsprings previously blocked by fractured intergenerational relationships between people, their families, and nations. They stem from roots of bitterness of families of generations past that, unchecked, will continue to lead to intergenerational rifts. They are like pearls made out of irritants in the sand, needing to be blown by the Spirit so treasures of destiny of nations intended from the beginning of time can come forth in this season. We need to take Jesus' healing love to the borders of the nations and redeem covenants of brotherly love.

Unity requires healing and restoration of historic bitter roots that caused the breach in relationships. This is why it is so critical to honor those who have gone before us, and repent of issues still unresolved. The healing love of God ministering to the root issues restores the tree of life and removes us from the curse of the tree of knowledge of good and evil. Iraqi Christian believers who live in the Garden of Eden, which long ago turned desert, say that for churches to survive in the Moslem world requires a spiritual vision of the demonstration of the power of the true God. Just as Jesus showed His authority with healing love, they need to see manifestation of His Kingdom, not rhetoric.

Abraham's son Ishmael felt cast out and rejected as Hagar was sent away with him. But God did open her eyes in the wilderness to see the life-giving spring of water to keep her and Ishmael from dying of thirst (see Gen. 21:14-19). The healing love of Father God for both sons would bring a heart to restore Ishmael and his generations back to the loving father Abraham for both sons. The root of bitterness needs the healing balm of Father God's love. We are in the season of the Son of God arising with healing in His wings to restore these relationships.

## The Righteous Reign

*"There shall come forth a Rod from the stem of Jesse, and a Branch shall grow out of his roots. The Spirit of the LORD shall rest upon Him"* (Isa. 11:1-2 NKJV). The first believers in Jesus were Jewish. They are referred to as the olive tree. Their roots were pure and holy. And their first-fruit faith spread among other national groups. Their faith made them part of God's tree of life. Their faithfulness to His covenants made them holy. If some branches were broken off by unfaithfulness (see Rom. 11:17), they were grafted in by faith when believers of other nations came to faith in the God of Abraham. To become a believer was to become part of the history and heritage of the believers. They are all grafted in to become part of God's olive tree. Our unifying element is to be grafted together as part of God's Tree of Life.

The message of Revelation is: "Hear what the Spirit says to the churches." John got his visions when he was seeing in the Spirit. It was the direct revelation of Jesus Christ. The Spirit of God opened his eyes and ears to hear the Spirit's message to the churches. Muslims are experiencing a similar phenomenon as Jesus is appearing to them to wake them up from their spiritual deadness. Having a healing ministry in Iraq, I spoke with Muslims who confessed they had a dream of the man in the white robe, wondering if it was really Jesus. They say when they have the dream that they see the fiery love in His eyes. They say their spirits are so drawn to Him that they are desperate to know how to get to Him. I tell them Jesus is personally calling them to come to Him, and they are so honored to be selected to come into His Kingdom. They are so smitten by His everlasting love as they feel His fiery heart of love to draw them that they want to be one with the believers. It causes us to want to be *as one.* His love is the laminin (glue) that holds us in the Body together. Scientifically, laminin holds our cellular structure together in our bodies, and spiritually Jesus' love holds the Body of Christ together.

Jesus' heart cry was that we would be one, that the world would see. And the fiery love of God rekindled in our hearts will bring that to fruition. Spiritual unity is the call of the hour. We must overcome our judgments of each other and come together to represent the Kingdom of God to the world. Unity comes as we worship and pray together. Our personal agendas don't seem so important when we are overcome by the bigger picture of His love that draws the world of believers together.

## Healing to the Nations

Our Healing Tree International ministry invests in the lives of leaders to bring an outflow of growth, vision, and resources to help the lives of needy people for God's redemptive healing of nations. We speak this destiny and vision into the lives of leaders so they will use their resources to bring God's purposes to fruition. We train, equip, and network leaders in various venues including roundtable destiny coaching and prayer meetings to bring a convergence of God's resources together for healing of nations. We address vision and destiny, medical and healing needs, social justice needs, pastoral care needs, and business and humanitarian needs in our country and developing countries. Our theme verse is Revelation 22:2: "The leaves of the trees bring healing to the nations" (paraphrased).

We are also state representatives connected with National Apostolic and Reformation Prayer Networks so we are positioned as part of the massive move of God converging ministries across the nation and nations. National prayer networks—uniting in stadiums, capitals, and churches—and worship concerts are bringing a massive cry to the Lord to bring His Kingdom on earth. God's people are worshiping, repenting, and ministering healing so many are moved with passion for the Kingdom. This is

God's heart: to see us radically worshiping and ministering with God's altar as the center. He is the one to be worshiped rather than a podium for one person.

Recently, as part of Cindy Jacobs Reformation Prayer Network Root 52, we gathered 60 intercessors representing churches and ministries across Pennsylvania to join together to pray forth the historic covenantal root of Pennsylvania, while all state prayer networks joined us in the prayer for Pennsylvania. This was to nurture William Penn's Seed of a Nation, which he envisioned to bring forth God's holy example of the peaceable kingdom to the nations. As we prayed and worshiped God, a bond of love was built between us. Our hearts wanted to bring healing to the breach between the First Nations who had been wronged by the English who came to take their land from them. After we prayed we asked First Nation Mohawk 3 Rivers council elder Gray Woolf what we needed to do to heal the breach that caused a bitter root in the injured First Nation people. He said they needed more than prayer initiatives. They needed honor restored and action to help them heal. They needed land. As he shared and we heard his need, the Lord built a love bond between us that stirred our hearts to give an offering to his people. By the end of the second day the Lord drew us to renew the covenant by lighting a unity candle and taking communion together. His heart was healed and he spread the word among his people.

This healing had ripple effects among the tribal people, and news came out in the tribal newspapers. The Lord healed a breach by His Spirit and began a new covenantal unity between us. By healing this ancient well, it opened up other ancient wells of relationships between Americans and immigrants coming to our land for freedom. It opened a door to healing as the holy seed of a nation planted in Pennsylvania can become a holy example to the nations.

We also took Penn's Charter to the Kurdish government to show them how God intended government to work with true freedom and justice for all. Kurdish government leaders then came to Pennsylvania to see this model that Penn established that there would be justice for all, and they too wanted to bring forth the holy model established by God for their people.

We are in a kairos time when God is redeeming His beloved back to Himself! He established a covenantal love and destiny for world dominion of His Kingdom with the first couple on earth in the intimacy of His Garden of Eden, at the beginning of time. Now He is rekindling in us His holy love to heal those covenantal roots. His grand scheme is restoration of His covenantal love with His beloved people. This everlasting love is drawing His people back to Himself, His generations stemming from the seed of Isaac and Ishmael. He is grafting together His people as the one new man, people who carry one spirit. The Spirit of God overcoming the breaches between people as His beloved Bride, the Church, is restoring her love for Him. It is His message of Revelation from the beginning of time.

Deuteronomy 32:8 says,

*When the Most High gave the nations their inheritance, when He separated the sons of man, He set the boundaries of the peoples according to the number of the sons of Israel* (NASB).

And Malachi 2:10 says,

*Do we not all have one father? Has not one God created us? Why do we deal treacherously each against his brother so as to profane the covenant of our fathers? (NASB)*

## His Peaceable Kingdom

Just as William Penn initiated a model of brotherly love and covenantal friendship at Penn Treaty Park for Pennsylvania, we need to establish Christian friendship between all people groups, and that will become a peaceable protection for all people to recognize the covenantal love of God's family all being one. Brother should not fight brother in the family of God!

## As One!

As one with the Spirit, the clarion call is: "The Spirit and the Bride say, *'Come!'*"

Each of us carry spiritual DNA seeds of God's destiny from the first moment God spoke to Adam and Eve and said to be fruitful and multiply and have dominion over all living things. God's everlasting love formed the first covenant of love and continues to call all people to Himself and to interdependence. Today He is calling the remnant of all the tribes of Israel back to Himself. His everlasting love has been the glue that has held us all together. There is a covenantal love root of all things that binds us to His everlasting love. He calls us to come back to that first love He established in the Garden. Restoring covenants of God is the "glia" glue that holds the holy family together. Restoring revival wells is restoring covenants of God. The Spirit and the Bride say, "*Come!* Come to the waters and enjoy the refreshing love of God even in the midst of uncertainties of the world. Come to Him. Come together. Love one another as He loves you!"

## Points to Ponder

1. What is the essential ingredient needed for the world to become one? What did Jesus pray about oneness and how could we join together to bring that about? See Jesus' final prayer for Himself, His disciples, and all believers in John chapter 17.

2. How do we bring healing between nations? How do we bring forth the holy purposes of the Ancient of Days? Jeremiah 31:3 (NKJV) says: *"I have loved you with an everlasting love...with lovingkindness I have drawn you."*

3. Whose job is it to impact nations for healing? What does the Great Commission mean for me? Matthew 28:19-20 (NKJV) says, *"Go...make disciples of all the nations...."*

CHAPTER 8

# Moses Is Dead—Time to Cross Over

## Dorsey Marshall

*Moses My servant is dead. Now then, you and all these people, get ready to cross the Jordan River into the land I am about to give to them...* (Joshua 1:2 NIV).

Recently my son and daughter-in-law were traveling out of town, and they asked my wife and me to keep our grandchildren and their dog, Barkley. Barkley is a typical, hyper Yorkshire Terrier. A Yorkie is a small dog with a big attitude. Everyone was getting ready to leave the house, and I overheard my granddaughter begging and pleading for Barkley to get into his crate. With his attitude, he was ignoring her, so with my deep authoritative voice, I commanded Barkley to get into his crate. He looked at me, turned completely away, and ignored me, too. I had no doubt that when my son returned home, command issues would be settled. Barkley would hear his master's voice, and it would be back to obedience once again.

Following the death of Moses and facing the task of conquering a land of fortified cities, Israel experienced a sense of hopelessness! However, trust and confidence in God will always restore hope in our lives. God is preparing, leading, and drawing us into a deeper relationship level than we have ever experienced. He is getting His Church ready, not just for the next level...but for a new dimension of walking with Him! Keep in mind, *"the Church"* is not the building we attend each week. *The Church is you and me!* Almighty God is getting us ready for a transition and transformation period by the power of the Holy Spirit.

In my early years I, *seemingly,* at least by example, learned that the infilling and baptism in the Holy Spirit was a result of being a good person. Being a good person is not a bad thing, but God baptizes us, not to reward us for being good, but to transform us, to change us, and to make us like Christ. This work of transformation will never happen through human assent; it is a work of God's grace in our lives.

The grace we speak of is more than the power to become born again; His grace is His daily operational power to accomplish anything to which He has called you. *"For by grace are ye saved through faith; and that not of yourselves: it is the gift of God"* (Eph. 2:8 KJV). That just gets you started! But what about after you are born again? Here is an example. You just do not slap a newly born baby on his behind, and say to him, "Son, you have it all now." That baby needs to grow, and so do you and I.

*According as His divine power hath given unto us all things that pertain unto life and godliness, through the knowledge of Him that hath called us to glory and virtue* (2 Peter 1:3 KJV).

## Remain Open to Change

Moses represents the old order of...doing-business-as-usual! Now, Moses is dead, and after spending 40 years in a desert wilderness with millions of doubting Israelites, God approached Joshua and told him to possess the land they had sought. The time had come to cross over into a new season of God's promises. Israel missed it when they left a land of bondage and slavery, while living in Egypt. They did not trust God's plan for their lives. I do not know about you, but I have missed a season or two in my life, but I will not miss every season in my life. A world-changer will be willing to leave the comfort of family, religion, and human tradition! You will not be a world-changer while you still think like the world.

God is sounding the trumpet through His prophets! The trumpet is a much larger instrument than the small piece that makes it work. The trumpet, constructed of brass, has tubing bent into an oblong shape. The shaping and bending of the brass creates a work of art for the master musician. It is the mouthpiece that actually makes all the sounds of this beautiful instrument. The remaining parts of the instrument spread its sound. Are you willing to be reshaped and bent for the purposes and plans of the Master?

It took 40 years in the wilderness wandering for the old nature of Israel to die. You and I have to die to the practices of humanism, rhetorical philosophy, arguments of men's minds, and religion for Christ to birth new life into our carnal, finite minds. He is an infinite God speaking to a finite people. The Word of the Lord to the Prophet has not changed.

*Then he answered and spake unto me, saying, This is the word of the Lord unto Zerubbabel, saying, Not by might, nor by power, but by My spirit, saith the LORD of hosts* (Zechariah 4:6 KJV).

God gave the vision to Joshua and Zerubbabel years later as they were restoring the temple in Judah after years of Babylonian captivity. God was telling them that their true source of power was not in human strength, but in the power of God.

## Never the Same, Again

God's desire is to change you and me. Are you ready for His Spirit to cut away the old flesh-nature, so you can walk in the demonstration and power of His calling in your life?

Change is not for the fainthearted. Change is also not an option for possessing all the promises He has for you. Like Israel, without a change in the way you think, do business, and live your life, you will wander in the wilderness of the paths you have chosen…and miss all that God has for you.

It is time for believers to transition out of the bondage and slavery of dead men's bones! Religion is dead! Religion does not work, but Jesus does. It is time for each of us to seek a full relationship with Jesus, the King, rather than what the Kingdom can do for us. Of course, there are benefits in the Kingdom, but if we will seek the King in a place of intimacy, He will withhold no good thing from us. It is time to break the 40-year cycle of going around the same mountain with no results. Albert Einstein said, "Insanity is doing the same thing over and over again and expecting different results." If you have not been receiving the desired result in your life, maybe it is time to try a different approach! If the things you have counted on and put your trust in have disappointed you, maybe they just might be dead, too! The greatest enemy to intimacy in any relationship is self-sufficiency.

Too many believers have memorialized certain ways of doing things. Jesus was speaking to the religious leaders of His day when He said, *"Making the word of God of no effect through your tradition which you have handed down. And many such things you do"* (Mark 7:13 NKJV). Religious rituals have replaced *manifestations* of the Holy Spirit and locked many in comfort zones that say, "This is how God does what He is going to do." Then, we spiritualize this heresy by assigning all the blame to God, and calling it, "The Sovereign Will of God."

We escape the responsibility of our own will by saying, "He is God; He is going to do what He wants to do, and I have no control over God. You know, He works in mysterious ways. Who can know the mind of God?" So, when God begins to move in a way that is different than what brought us in, there is a natural tendency to resist Him because it just does not fit our religious architecture. Well, if you will look at what He really said in His revealed Word, you will see a different picture about knowing the mind of God. Paul gave this instruction to the very carnal Corinthians: *"For who hath known the mind of the Lord, that he may instruct Him? But we have the mind of Christ"* (1 Cor. 2:16 KJV).

## It's More Than Church!

God is calling His true worshipers and followers to a place of holiness. If we are not careful, we will even make holiness a big, fancy churchy and religious concept. Holiness is not a church concept; it is a way of life. Holiness is separating yourself from anything and anyone that will keep you from hearing the Lord. If the people in your life are not increasing you, they will eventually decrease you! In this hour of moving into the full promises of God, you and I need to spend more time in His presence, not doing the same thing we have done all of our lives.

Many of God's people spend time with God complaining, as the Israelites did, and then call it prayer. God is calling you and me to a place of intimacy where we go into the *Most Holy Place*, the throne room. It is a place beyond man's *veil* or wall of separation from God. Jesus tore down that wall. Holy Spirit is leading God's people beyond man's limitations, man's religious order, and escorting a people of desire into the place where we just sit at His feet...in His presence...hearing Him.

We must remember, satan has a voice and speaks quite well. Just like the story I mentioned earlier about my son's family dog, Barkley, not every voice you hear is the Master's voice. That brings us to a question we all ask, "How can I know I am hearing the voice I should listen to?" The Bible is clear about that subject; we are to measure the voice we hear according to God's Word. In First John 4:1-3, the writer says that we are to *"...test the spirits to see whether they are from God..."* (NASB). John goes on to say that there are many who claim to have authority and speak as the voice of God, but they speak from a world system view. They are not from God. They are speaking to fulfill their own interest and for their own benefit. The true test to know, for certain, that what you hear is from the Master is in verse 2 of this text, *"This is how you can recognize the Spirit of God: Every spirit that acknowledges that Jesus Christ has come in the flesh is from God..."* (1 John 4:2 NIV).

Measure the voice you hear with these thoughts: First, it must agree with the Bible. Second, it must make you more like Jesus. Third, you should have confirmation with other believers. Fourth, it should be consistent with the way God has been shaping you. Fifth, it must include your involvement. If it does not include you, why would God speak to you about it? Sixth, it should bring conviction, not condemnation. Seventh, it must bring God's peace.

God is calling out to you, my friend. He is saying, *"My people, hear My teaching; listen to the words of My mouth"* (Ps. 78:1 NIV). Like Israel, many have heard the voice of God many times, but their hearts have grown cold. Let us never become like the Israelites. They were *religious*, but without *relationship* with the Master. Let us build and maintain an *intimacy* with God, where we lay our head upon His chest and hear His heartbeat. Then, let us learn to think like Him.

Welcome a fresh walk with the Master into your life today! There is something new being birthed in you. Keep an ear ready; He is speaking to you about moving into the land of promise, into a place of intimacy with Him.

## Points to Ponder

1. Are you ready to think differently for a "change"? Are you willing to let the Holy Spirit be your guide?

2. Your weakness is in the hands of a healthy God! Can you accept your own vulnerability and allow yourself to be weak so that He can demonstrate His strength?

3. Are you open to His ways? Are you willing to forsake your ways and enter into a place of intimacy with the Father?

# CHAPTER 9

# Intimate Ecstasies

## Doug Alexander

*My heart is overflowing with a good theme; I recite my composition concerning the King; my tongue is the pen of a **ready writer*** (Psalm 45:1 NKJV).

The Spirit of God is energizing the scribal anointing in the earth, as evidenced by the film, *The Book of Eli*. Denzel Washington's character, as Eli, embarks on a journey westward across a barren, post-apocalyptic wilderness. Eli's heroic mission, inspired by God, is to preserve the last Bible left on earth and take it to a safe archive. The honoring of God's Word is a recurring theme throughout. Eli stewards the Word by hiding it in his heart and later transcribing it, as the psalmist described, with a *"tongue [that] is the pen of a ready writer"* (Ps. 45:1; cross reference Ps. 119:11; Luke 2:19).

The movie reveals the adversary, Carnegie, as a type of antichrist, who attempts to steal the only remaining Bible on the planet so he can manipulate the world through a religious spirit of deception. He wants to exploit the sacred Book that Eli is carrying and use it for self gain. God uses Eli to prevent this demonic takeover of the planet. Eli prays and meditates on the Book day and night. He becomes so consumed by the Spirit of Truth that he is able to walk by faith and not by sight, literally! (See Second Corinthians 5:7.) This equips him with the supernatural prowess to defeat the various enemies Carnegie sends to intercept the book. Eli stays within God's protective hedge due to a diligent devotion to the Book and a close relationship with the Author.

This motion picture could be interpreted as a prophetic portrait of the Body of Christ—the New Creation Man foreshadowed in Psalm 45. This many-membered postmodern warrior, carrying the ancient Word, is a fallen world's only hope after being devastated by darkness and incinerated by sin. It is a dusty land, nuked by iniquity and inundated with ignorance of the ancient truths. The only thing that can save such a world is Christ in and amongst us, imparting healing virtue to a diseased and decadent world. The movie illustrates how the world is changed through the faithfulness and skill of a devoted scribe.

According to John 1, Jesus Christ is *"the Word made flesh"* (see verses 1 and 14). The Church, also known as the Body of Christ, participates in this same ongoing incarnation. Believers partake of the divine nature by receiving *"the exceedingly great and precious promises"* of God (2 Pet. 1:4) and incorporating them into their daily lives. This internal empowerment is what qualifies God's people to revolutionize the world around them.

## The Sword of the Spirit

One attribute of the divine nature within is that of a mighty conquering warrior. Our Messiah is the Master Swordsman of the Spirit. Following a 40-day fast, when Jesus faced the devil in the desert, He only used one weapon. To every temptation Jesus responded with *"it is written"* from the Scriptures (see Luke 4). He lived under an open heaven and read from an open book. He kept His spiritual sword sharp by "studying to show Himself approved," just as Paul exhorted his spiritual son Timothy to do (see 2 Tim. 2:15). This is how our Messiah grew throughout His upbringing in "favor, wisdom and stature" (see Luke 2:52).

At the end of His life, Jesus quoted the 22nd Psalm verbatim as He hung on the cross in His ultimate battle for the salvation of mankind. Thank God the demonic powers were defeated that day, and we can now live from Calvary's victory, enjoying the spoils of His finished work. We who have been co-crucified with Him now reign together as joint heirs with our resurrected Master who has a *"sharper than any two edged sword"* blazing from His mouth…dividing darkness from light, and the lower carnal realm from the higher spiritual dimension of His Life.

Throughout the aforementioned movie, Eli stays in the Book. He also demonstrates a vigilant mastery with his sword around adversaries. God's new creation people are advised by Paul to exhibit the same skillfulness and allow this Warrior within to bear His mighty sword through our confrontations with the (lower) powers of darkness:

> *In conclusion, be strong in the Lord [be **empowered through your union with Him**]; draw your strength from Him [that strength which His boundless might provides]. Put on God's whole armor [the armor of **a heavy-armed soldier** which God supplies], that you may be able successfully to stand up against [all] the strategies and the deceits of the devil....And take the helmet of salvation and the **sword that the Spirit wields, which is the Word of God** [The Message version says: God's Word is an indispensable weapon]* (Ephesians 6:10-11,17 AMP).

The Old Testament is loaded with references to this mighty Warrior King as well. Here are a couple:

> *When I sharpen My lightning sword and execute judgment, I take vengeance on My enemies and pay back those who hate Me* (Deuteronomy 32:41 MSG).

> *Warrior, strap Your sword at Your thigh; gird on Your splendor and majesty* (Psalm 45:3 Complete Jewish Bible).

## A Divine Romance

God waged war on our enemies to establish a lasting peace. Keep in mind that our opponents are not flesh and blood (human beings). Our heavenly King may be a mighty fighter, but even more so our Warrior Lord is a great lover. The aim of this spiritual violence is to bring us into the tranquility of matrimonial bliss. Psalm 45 is an epic panorama of the romance between humanity and deity. It rivals even The Song of Songs between the Shulamite and King Solomon in its scope. Psalm 45 prophetically foreshadows the New Covenant Church wooed by the King's tender touch into full submission as His Eternal Bride in the ultimate love story of the ages. This whole passage embodies how to get in touch with the Creator, tap into His creativity, and in turn touch the rest of creation. It's a majestic psalm that paints a picture of interactive Kingdom life and what it means to engage with Perfect Love Himself…in all His resplendent glory.

*My heart bursts its banks, spilling beauty and goodness.*
*I pour it out in a poem to the king, shaping the river*
*into words* (Psalm 45:1 MSG).

A river of Life flowing from the Throne of Heaven is bursting its banks in the corporate heart of the Body of the Anointed One. The intimate ecstasies of individuals, enthralled with their King, are converging into one body of living water. This curse-free creation is wildly celebrating with holy abandon. The greatest, happiest party of all time is breaking forth! A rush of bliss-saturated poetry, brimming with (zoe-filled) divine life, is coursing through a people who are beside themselves with adoration. These mighty rivers of living water can no longer be contained in the confines of the human heart. The out-flowing "zoetry" is a spontaneous art form that originates from the indwelling Creator. These floodwaters are coming soon to a neighborhood near you.

No one in his right mind would argue that the world doesn't need to be changed. This cannot be achieved politically or by the hand of man. Nonetheless the world *must* be changed for the better—and not just a makeover. It needs a complete Kingdom takeover! It is begging for a lasting change from the roots up.

The good news is that this world *will* be changed beyond recognition as the dams burst and this raging river starts rolling. This ecstatic move will not just come and go as another visitation of revival. It is no less than the permanent habitation of God's presence permeating planet Earth. Psalm 45 is a dynamic illustration of how this mega-reformation will transpire. This transformation is conceived in a simple love song as our Beloved woos us into the chambers of His innermost Being.

## A Scribal Activation

God is draping the mantle of a "ready writer" on His Body in these end times. The earth needs the Spirit of Truth like never before. The Lord recently whispered in my spirit,

*"I'm activating a strong anointing in My people to release a bardic YALP to the nations. A Psalm 45 activation is at hand. It will enable them to ride the high places and suck sweet honey from the Rock and draw oil out of the Scriptures. This activation will quicken their tongues to speak the oracles of God as the pen of a ready writer."*

This corporate movement can only be ignited through an intimate relationship with the Author and Finisher of our faith. So what exactly then is a "*bardic yalp*"?

In the Celtic tradition, a "bard" is defined as: "A person who composed and recited epic or heroic poems, often while playing an instrument. Any poet" (Encarta World English Dictionary). No one has a more epic story to show and tell, than the people who've come into league with the greatest superhero of all time: Jesus—the King of Glory (see Ps. 24). A bardic anointing to articulate who He is—through prose, poetry, and a plethora of other artistic expressions—has been triggered in this era. This good news (Gospel) of nothing less than the invasion of Heaven on earth will result in a creative renaissance and a festival of planetary jubilee!

The "yalp" can represent the archetypal battle cry of the warrior intercessor (see Isa. 58:1). It is like a travailing mother giving birth to new life (see Isa. 54:1; 66:7-8). It can also be likened to the enslaved Israelites making their mass exodus from Egypt into the land of promise after Moses commanded of Pharaoh: *"Let my people go"!* (See Exodus 5:1.) God heard their cry. This "yalp" is undoubtedly the Pauline description (in Romans 8) of the entire creation groaning in anticipation—of the promised unveiling of the fully formed sons of God—who finally rid earth of the curse originally broken at Calvary's cross.

Paul's YALP:

*My little children, for whom I am again suffering* **birth pangs** *until Christ is completely and permanently formed (molded) within you* (Galatians 4:19 AMP).

Job painted the following word picture of this spiritual out bursting of our inner man:

*For I am full of words; the spirit within me compels me. Indeed my belly is like wine that has no vent; it is ready to burst like new wineskins. I will speak, that I may find relief; I must open my lips and answer* (Job 32:18-20 NKJV).

The sound of this strategic "yalp" can also be heard throughout popular culture:

I too am not a bit tamed, I too am untranslatable,
I sound my barbaric YAWP over the roofs of the world. –Walt Whitman, "Leaves of Grass"

In the movie, *The Dead Poets Society*, when the unconventional teacher Mr. Keating (played by Robin Williams) provokes his shy student Todd (played by Ethan Hawke) to emote his own "barbaric YAWP," the result is pure liberation. Todd is loosed from the shackles of societal conformity and personal intimidation that had him subdued. His inner poet busts loose with newfound passion. He discovers the fire in his belly.

In the Dr. Seuss classic *Horton Hears a Who*, the Mayor of Whoville advises little Jojo:

> "We've GOT to make noises in greater amounts!
> So, open your mouth, lad! For every voice counts!"
> Thus he spoke as he climbed. When they got to the top,
> The lad cleared his throat and he shouted out, "YOPP!"
> And that Yopp...That one small, extra Yopp put it over!
> Finally, at last! From that speck on that clover
> Their voices were heard! They rang out clear and clean.
> And the elephant smiled. "Do you see what I mean?...
> They've proved they ARE persons, no matter how small.
> And their whole world was saved by the smallest of All!"[1]

Somehow a sound barrier is broken by this primitive groan, or yalp, if you will. From our inarticulate cry something happens in the heavens (see Rom. 8:26; 1 Cor. 14:14-15). Out of weakness and suffering strength arises. Understanding also comes. This breaking of the sound barrier opens up an articulation of fresh wisdom. Grace answers the groan. Dr. Kelley Varner called it "the groan from the Throne" and often said, "You are an original. There is no one uniquely made like you, who can say it quite like you can say it." So don't delay, discover your individual yalp! This is just another strange way God uses the foolish things to confound the wise.

## Speaking From the Most Holy Place

A "ready writer" who has "touched the King" taps the inner voice. He is not only "ready" to right the wrongs in his own thinking but starts to shine brightly on the kingdom of darkness around him. This "ready writer" becomes *"instant in season and out of season,"* having discovered the secret of abiding—of remaining continually refreshed in his relationship with God.

The principle that Paul shared in the Book of Romans that *"faith comes by hearing,"* can only happen by a devoted listening in the present tense—which releases a fresh sense of God's presence every time one speaks and hears. Romans 10:17 doesn't say faith comes by **having heard** (in the past tense). The apostle Peter wrote about being *"established in the **present** truth"* (1 Pet. 1:12). The word in that verse translated "present" is the word *pareimi*, which means: "to be by, be at hand, to have arrived, to be present, to **be ready**, in store, at command, be here, **be present here**, come, **in the moment**."[2] Present truth connects us to His presence. The present moment is the eternal gift that keeps on giving. That's probably why it is called "the present." There is only the ever-present and eternal "now"—where we become current with whatever He is speaking to us today and thus enter into His sabbath rest, if we mix His words with faith (see Heb. 4).

There is always a "right now" word from the I AM (not "I was," or "I will be..."). Our "right now" God keeps talking to us in the present. We must "be here now" ever ready with Jehovah Shammah (the "Lord is There" = means *here!*), sensitized to His "still small voice"—every moment...day after day. Silence also speaks volumes (it really is golden!). To *"be still"* is how we come to *"know God"* intimately (see Ps. 46:10).

We also learn to behold His beauty and awe in the natural world, as it too preaches the Gospel—without ever uttering words (see Rom. 1:20). Creation reveals the artistry and attributes of the Creator. Nature unveils the divine nature. The omnipresent Creator manifests in space and time when we approach Him with open hearts, eyes, and ears—ready to engage with Him at all times.

Paul guarantees that faith comes only through hearing *and* hearing and hearing. It is a continual ongoing place of hearing His Word in the present. We can't live off yesterday's meal. We live by every word that *proceeds* out of the mouth of God now, not the preceding words...the *"proceeding"* Word is what keeps us moving forward (see Matt. 4:4). Static faith is death. Yesterday's manna is rotten and riddled with worms (see Exod. 16:18-20).

There's a breakfast of heavenly baked manna awaiting us every morning, prompting the age-old question: "*what is it*"? Manna causes us to inquire of the Father and, with the inner aid of the Holy Spirit, to solve the hidden mysteries. Greater understanding comes as we develop this lifestyle of divine inquiry.

We "touch" the King when our attention is riveted on Him, attending or inclining to His words (see Prov. 4:1-13). This unbroken focus is one of the major ways we embrace the Lord and bring Him pleasure. It is impossible to please God without faith (see Heb. 11:6). When we learn to listen, God actually "creates a hearing ear" (see Prov. 20:12). His creative voice implants seeds of new life to germinate in us and generate fresh thinking and vision. A genesis happens!

The prophet Jeremiah spoke about "separating the precious from the profane" to remain His mouthpiece (see Jer. 15:19). I've learned over time to search for the sacred in the secular, to not run scared from it. His omniscience is everywhere if we really believe He is everywhere (omnipresent). In other words the knowledge of God is available in every situation at all times. Wisdom actually cries in the streets day and night to be heard (see Prov. 8).

He is always speaking. There is a massive feast of truth available to all, yet Amos warned about a "*famine of the hearing of the Word.*" We shouldn't just listen for God when we hear a sermon or read the Bible. The mind of Christ "instructs" in every situation (see 1 Cor. 2:16). Whether I'm watching an episode of *Lost* on television, looking at a billboard driving down the road, listening to a rock song on the radio, talking to a friend, or a colleague, a client, or supervisor, or just chilling with my family, I keep listening carefully (see Mark 4:24) for that Voice within the voice. I stay dialed to His station, tuned into His heart and mind, surrounded by His counsel...expecting fresh revelation. Poet Robert Hunter put it this way: "Once in a while you get shown the light in the strangest of places if you look at it right" (from the song, "Scarlet Begonias").

After we have been turned onto the Lord and have touched the King, He turns up the volume. Thus we become individual channels of His Voice and unique expressions of His person. What possibilities. What a life! Endless epiphanies await us. Now He may speak through me as a "ready writer." Simply because I'm tuned in, He is able to first broadcast *to* me, and then *through* me. I become a mobile radio station of Heaven in my regular daily walk, transmitting rarefied sound waves from the other side. The ordinary life becomes extraordinary—beaming the Kingdom of Heaven to every sphere of influence I have. When we communicate from this transcendent realm of communion, real Life begins to happen. A person's spirit literally transforms into His Holy of Holies on the ground—empowering him to *"speak as the oracles of God"* (1 Pet. 4:11 NKJV).

This scribal "activation" is a tsunami starter, the catalyst of a prophetic wave of unparalleled proportions. It breaks down the barrier that has long existed between Christian and popular culture at large. It is not an invasion of overzealous Bible thumpers, but an infiltration of divine trumpeters who exhibit both a compassionate sensitivity and supernatural power. Bob Jones says that the greatest bait on our fishing hook is the glory. The splendor of Heaven emanating from God's people draws this world into His Kingdom like nothing else.

However this tidal wave manifests, it will not reek with the stench of dry religion but rather an aroma of heavenly wisdom that is peaceable and irrefutable. We are spiritually born from above by the Word of truth (see James 1:17-18). The living Word is also the spiritual milk that enables us to grow (see 1 Pet. 2:2). God's kids must learn to live and speak the Word till the things which are not have become a tangible reality (see Rom. 4:17). The invisible and impossible promises are rendered visible and entirely possible as we boldly proclaim and consistently confess them.

The past 40 years the Body of Christ has been taught the power of the spoken word and how to move mountains through the power of life and death that is resident in the tongue (see Mark 11:23; Prov. 18:21). This was not meant to just get our personal needs met. We are now being released from the four walls of the buildings that contained us and compelled outward to move the mountains that have been in the way. Our expression will become culturally relevant in the marketplace among non-believers without compromising one iota of Kingdom truth or love. The spoken word has corporate purpose foremost.

Out of my belly (innermost being) flows a fountain of living waters! (See John 7:38.) Out of this "common union" between man and God, we encourage and feed one another with the "commonwealth" of our mutual inheritance. Bill Johnson has described it as sharing a slice of bread from your own loaf. This isn't coming up with clever sermon ideas to impress people. It is ministering His Life through our lives! Talk about a state of grace! This condition of inner union makes sharing our faith with others an effortless delight. Nothing is forced. It just "oozes" out by impartation and never comes off as stale, didactic, or judgmental. This form of communion is relational and utterly relevant. Fun, even. And world-changing at the same time!

## The Sound of a Most Holy Place People

> *Do you not discern and understand that you...are God's temple (His sanctuary), and that God's Spirit has His permanent dwelling in you [to be at home in you, collectively as a church and also individually]?* (1 Corinthians 3:16 AMP)

As His sanctuary, we begin individually as an actual Holy of Holies (a mobile Most Holy Place) transporting the Ark of the Covenant in our spirit being, transmitting His same Spirit into the atmosphere. Our environment can be sanctified to the point of becoming a most holy place! When we assemble with others we comprise a collective temple of the Spirit, a superstructure habitation. From the threshold of our inner chambers the living waters flow to the outer courts of the surrounding world. The spiritual journey in Psalm 45 begins with a "touch" and extends into full possession, since we are not our own and have been bought with a price (see 1 Cor. 6:20). God takes full ownership as the rightful Lord of our lives. His glory transcends the universe with the celestial sounds of Heaven.

> *To the Chief Musician, Concerning the Lilies. For the sons of Korah. A Poem; a Song of the Beloved. My heart is overflowing with a good matter. I am speaking of my works to the King; my tongue is the pen of a rapidwriter* (Psalm 45:1 Green's Literal Translation).

Jesus Christ is the Chief Musician. He conducts the symphony and directs the choir. He is both the Song and the Chief Singer. He is the lion of the Tribe of Judah (*Judah* = "Praise") roaring out of Zion. He is the Heavenly David playing the stringed instruments that drives the forces of darkness off of Saul (who typifies the demonized *soul*). Jesus also personifies the music of Heaven. He is the Song of songs in the Most Holy Place. In the overflow of our hearts comes a new song radiating the high praises of God.

> *So sing, Daughter Zion! Raise the rafters, Israel! Daughter Jerusalem, be happy! celebrate! God has reversed His*

*judgments against you and sent your enemies off chasing their tails. From now on, God is Israel's king, in charge at the center. There's nothing to fear from evil ever again! Jerusalem will be told: "Don't be afraid. Dear Zion, don't despair. Your God is present among you, a strong Warrior there to save you. Happy to have you back, He'll calm you with His love and delight you with His songs"* (Zephaniah 3:14-17 MSG).

The New King James version put it this way:

*The LORD your God in your midst, the Mighty One, will save; He will rejoice over you with gladness, He will quiet you with His love,* ***He will rejoice over you with singing*** (Zephaniah 3:17 NKJV).

The universal language of music transcends every culture. God has hidden Himself in every form of music and can be discovered singing and rejoicing over His Beloved. The Song of Songs streaming from the Holy of Holies may be heard if you are listening. It is one of the main keys that will open a door to changing the nations.

There are "God winks" throughout the music of popular culture and among every tribe and tongue. God continually sings over His creation. Psalm 45:1 is also called "The Song of the Beloved." The first eight verses unveil the King (the Redeemer deity) in all His glory and the final nine verses reveal His Bride the Queen (redeemed humanity).

## "The Song of Loves" Touching the King

The 45th Psalm, a royal offering of praise, has also been titled "The Song of Loves." The "ready writers" of verse 1 do not speak so much out of *what* they know, but from *who* they know. Change can only happen after a people have "touched the King." The catalyst to a global transformation of Heaven on earth is intimate contact between individuals and their Maker. Once we have "touched the King" and received His touch in return, we can then "pay it forward" and touch others. This is how the world is transformed—one testimony at a time. The anointed touch of His Body nudges humanity into His proximity...and into a close encounter with the King.

The Potter's Hand that forms the clay is part of His Anointed Body. The leadership role of the fivefold ministry (of apostles, prophets, evangelists, pastors, and teachers enumerated in Ephesians 4:11—the fingers, if you will) is the hand that helps mold clay pots into vessels of honor. Now the Holy Spirit can fill these containers with His presence and continually pour out of them and refresh the land.

What a touch it is! The Hebrew word for "touching [the King]" in Psalm 45 can be translated, joined, to select.[3] Being "joined" to the King brings us into union, the new birth described in John chapter 3 that allows us to see and enter the Kingdom. First Corinthians 6:17 in the Amplified Bible says: *"But the person who is united to the Lord becomes one spirit with Him."* That same verse in the King

James Version says: *"But he that is joined unto the Lord is one spirit."* The word "joined" in the Greek is *kollao*, it means to glue together, cement, to join or fasten firmly together, to join one's self to, cleave to, associate, cling.[4] We have been attached, bone to His Bone, flesh of His Flesh! As one New Man, He is the Head—we are the Body. When someone enters a room we don't say, "There's Joe's head and his body." They are one and the same. We are joined to the Head. He is the Vine; we are the branches. We have been grafted into the same Tree of Life to grow leaves that heal the nations and fruit that tastes of His surpassing grace and perfect nature.

Union with Jesus ignites the very fire and spirit of true prophetic ministry. It is not necessarily predictive, although foretelling and bringing the future into the present is one aspect of the prophetic. The primary essence or core "spirit of prophecy is the testimony of Jesus" (see Rev. 19:10). Testimony is simply giving evidence. It's a personal power encounter that is firsthand, not hearsay. It comes from being an eyewitness, through experiential knowledge...and is then presented in the court of public opinion. As eyewitnesses who have touched the King we become qualified to give the testimony of a "ready writer."

A detailed devotional study of Psalm 45 yields great rewards. Many nuggets can be excavated. Great insight is available through in-depth exegesis, but an aerial overview of the high points also has illuminating returns. It starts in verse 1 in the throes of personal intimacy with the King and ends 17 verses later in a multigenerational blessing as the Kingdom of Heaven on earth.

*I will bring honor to Your name in every generation. Therefore, the nations will praise You forever and ever* (Psalm 45:17 NLT).

## Accepted in the Beloved

Psalm 45 is also called "The Song of the Beloved." The apostle Paul wrote to the church at Ephesus: *"To the praise of the glory of His grace, wherein He hath made us accepted in the beloved"* (Eph. 1:6 KJV).

To change society in a lasting way, we must learn how to *"be loved."* This is an ongoing position of being loved inside and out. God is Love. To know Him is to love *Him.* He first loved us. The Person of God is pure love. Nothing can separate us from this unconditional covenantal love that is even stronger than death. We can either receive or reject it.

Love is the "Royal Law of the Kingdom." As disciples we must not turn from the "greatest of these" (see 1 Cor. 13:13), or step down from this highest dimension of the Kingdom. John the Revelator rebuked the church at Ephesus for "leaving their first love" (see Rev. 2:4). Somehow they had fallen from that place of amazing grace in their acceptance as God's beloved. This high station must be sustained.

One thing is certain—we will never be able to maintain first love passion by our own strength. To fulfill the greatest commandment (of loving God with all your heart, soul, mind, and strength) and keep the fires of "first love" stoked, we must learn to continually receive this God of love and all He is giving to us. Ultimately I must conclude: "I can't do it, but He can through me!" The main thing I have to do is give Him the reins.

It's actually an impossible task to walk in love—unless you have yielded to Perfect Love Himself. The second greatest commandment is loving your neighbor as yourself. There it is again. To let God love others through my personality and life I must first understand His passion for me. If I don't love myself (with God's love) and see through the prism of God's love for me, I will be incapable of truly loving others. The compassion that should move my heart for another comes from the passion God has freely shown toward me.

I can only fulfill "the great commission" to go into all the world with this good news (see Matt. 28) if I am rooted and grounded in love and saturated in the sense of a "greatest commandment" consciousness. The great commission is made possible as we obey the great commandments (loving God and others). The "greater works" Jesus promised we would do are contingent upon *His* "finished work" at Calvary. We can build on that foundation. His undying love is communicated through the cross. That's the floor we can dance upon. His finished work is our beginning. The miraculous is made easy and the supernatural is simplified when

I have soaked in all that God has done to redeem man. The divine romance becomes a reality. Real living comes out of *be*ing. In this restful place of being I can *"be loved"* and distribute it to others.

## An Aerial Overview of the 45th Psalm

This first verse of Psalm 45 fixes the focus of this company of ready writers on their King. Of course the actual psalm predates the earthly ministry of Jesus, yet it eloquently reveals the bridal mindset His Church is supposed to wear in the earth. This mentality is a paradigm designed to crown her thinking as Mrs. Jesus Christ—Queen of Glory.

Jesus came preaching "seek the Kingdom first" (see Matt. 6:33). His central message was *"Repent (change your mind); the Kingdom of Heaven is at hand."* The King of a new evil-free world had arrived and brought an order to His subjects to change their thinking and receive this higher Kingdom...and He brought a new government with Him.

The realm of Heaven is now within reach. We first touch the King and then extend our hands and impart His dominion to others. Jesus taught His disciples to pray to God the Father: *"...Your will be done on earth as it is in Heaven"* (Matt. 6:10). As we make contact with the King we become channels for the Kingdom of Heaven to come through our earthly measures of rule. This is how Heaven invades earth in this present world age.

Verse 1 of Psalm 45 also speaks of *"inditing a good matter"* (KJV). The Gospel of the Kingdom is all about the good news of higher authority ridding earth of the curse and restoring the blessing of Eden. This divine occupation is accelerated through prayer. This kind of communication is not just praying in the understanding of your native language. It is praying in the spirit—in your new heavenly language—speaking divine mysteries that unravel God's perfect will as we minister to Him in a place of intimacy. This is not a performance-driven form of ministry. It is a Kingdom-ruled, presence-driven lifestyle. It is *not* a repetitive religious form of prayer but anointed praying initiated from the throne. A royal priesthood is arising up from the earthly into the heavenly realms, ever advancing the Kingdom of God amid the kingdoms of men.

As this great awakening dawns, a brave company of reformers is on the rise. This group of "rapid writing" ecstatic scribes are *riding* the waves while *writing* the waves. Just as Habakkuk foretold, they *"write the vision and make it plain so all may run with it"* (see Hab. 2:2) as Good News warriors of the Kingdom. They are transfigured into the same image because they are transfixed by the King's beauty. Just as Eli was empowered with God's Word, the scribal mantle on the New Creation Man will deliver a generation from this present darkness.

Face to face communion with the King of Glory causes this company to see, and opens their ears to hear the sweet sound from His "lips of grace" (see Ps. 45:2). They realize the

Gospel is Good News that makes people healthy and happy, not a message of judgment and imminent doom and gloom. They believe God came to save the world—not to condemn it! This breed of bold new mystics is not contaminated by outward shows of religiosity. They are not "do it yourself" members of a morality club. Instead, they access an unlimited measure of grace by simply believing what He says and feeding on the communal bread (body) and wine (blood) of Christ.

These ecstatics are beside themselves with the new wine of the Spirit—free of dead works because they base their whole life and ministry on His finished work. They are seated together with Him in heavenly places, laughing at the spoiling of every principality and power. They share in the *"oil of gladness"* that anoints their King (Ps. 45:7 KJV). It is an unspeakable joy, full of glory. Their holy happiness results in a joyful mega-trend that continually strengthens them and is spreading like a wildfire throughout the world. This infectious hilarious movement is an unending glory party of mammoth proportions. Their cheer will even carry them through times of great trouble. The pressure of perilous times will not rob them of their praises.

This anointing also results in a spotless bride, the royal daughter who is *"all glorious within"* (described in Psalm 45:13). Her identification is based on who Christ already is within. Galatians 2:20 is her reality. She has been crucified with Christ and has been replaced by Christ Himself. Through identification with Him, a Most Holy Place people emerges. They are a brand-new species of beings, created in His image.

This daughter's clothing is of *"wrought gold"* (also *"interwoven* [NASB] *with gold"*) (see Ps. 45:13), which speaks of the divine nature displayed without. She has been formed and fashioned into His likeness, and it shows. The sufferings of Christ have disclosed a weightier glory that rests upon her. This golden apparel represents the Church putting *on* Christ and wearing Him outwardly. Christ *in* us becomes Christ *as* us...as we move to greater levels of manifest glory.

A day is soon coming when the church will demonstrate maturity as the fully seasoned sons (male and female) of God, unveiled to all creation. Our gifts and fruit will have ripened enough for the nations of the earth to eat. The earth groans and travails for that day to arrive. Indeed a barbaric yawp is sounding forth in the world! The Feast of Tabernacles will be celebrated fully as the nations rejoice that God is tabernacling in and among His people. It will take the whole church to change the whole world. Believing and experiencing the full Gospel of the Kingdom is paramount to this happening—in earth as it is in Heaven.

## Points to Ponder

1. Read the following summary of Psalm 45. Meditate and pray about what these things mean in your life.

   A. Intimacy—"touching the King" (from verse 1). We must come into intimate contact with the King until we are enjoying full union as His beloved. This change of thinking will cause us to enter into the Kingdom of Heaven right here in the earth.

   B. Grace—"lips of grace" (from verse 2). The Gospel is good news about His finished work on the cross. His amazing grace means the end of our religious dead works.

   C. Joy—"oil of gladness" (from verse 7). An ecstatic movement of unspeakable joy is spreading across the earth and empowering the people of God with His strength.

   D. Christ within—"all glorious within" (from verse 13). Through identification with Christ a Most Holy Place people are emerging. They are a brand-new species of being created in His image. This speaks of Christ *in* us.

   E. Christ upon—"clothing is of wrought gold" or "interwoven" (from verse 13). The manifest sons of God are a mature people who have been so formed and fashioned in Him that they now "wear" Christ upon their lives and ministries. They display both His power and character in royal array. This speaks of Christ *as* us.

2. Take a few moments to consider the following three world-changer principles from Psalm 45:1:

A. Activation of the Scribal Anointing: God is increasing the scribal anointing in His People to honor His Word and restore the spirit of truth in the earth. The religious spirit of deception will be driven out as we connect with the Book and come to know the Author. The Church is being exhorted by God to become people of the Book again.

B. Touching the King: We must enter into such intimate and holy contact with the King until we have touched His heart and He has touched ours and all those around us. A great impartation is transpiring between God and His people.

C. Acceptance in the Beloved: To impart the fullness of His presence on earth, we must realize our acceptance as His beloved. *We* can achieve the Great Commission and fulfill the second greatest commandment ("love your neighbor as yourself") if we stoke the fervent fires of our first love. Compassion for others will flow out of this passion for Him.

3. What does this mean to *you*? Ask God what He wants you to learn from this chapter and then spend some

time journaling what it is that you hear Him speaking to you.

## Endnotes

1. Dr. Seuss, *Horton Hears a Who* (New York: Random House, 1954).

2. Greek Lexicon; http://www.searchgodsword.org/lex/grk/view.cgi?number=3918; accessed October 11, 2010.

3 Greek Lexicon; http://www.searchgodsword.org/lex/grk/view.cgi?number=680; accessed October 11, 2010.

4 Greek Lexicon; http://www.searchgodsword.org/lex/grk/view.cgi?number=681; accessed October 11, 2010.

# CHAPTER 10

# *The Secret Place*

## Lisa Jo Greer

Where do world-changers come from? They come from spending time alone with the Lord. They come from the Secret Place. Intimacy is a mark of a world-changer, and intimacy can only come from time spent alone with Him. Matthew 6:6 is a key verse for a world-changer. It states: *"But when you pray, go into your room, close the door and pray to your Father, who is unseen. Then your Father, who sees what is done in secret, will reward you"* (NIV). How is intimacy cultivated? Jesus Himself teaches us this in Matthew 6:6.

First, intimacy begins with privacy. We are told to go into our room and close the door. The Lord knows that in order to have intimacy with us, there must be privacy. We are to go to the privacy of our room. This, for many of us, could be our bedroom, but it could also be any room in our home where we know that we will not be disturbed. It could be an attic, a bathroom, even a downstairs office. We are then told to shut the door. Why are we to shut the door? We are told to shut the door because the Lord does not want us to be interrupted in our time with Him. He knows that if we don't shut the door, others could intrude upon His precious time spent with us. The Lord is a jealous God, and He does not want anything or anyone interrupting His time. Shutting the door does not just mean shutting a physical door it also means shutting out the distractions of the day (i.e., family members, television, radio, e-mail, our cell phones, i-Pods, and the list goes on). The Lord does not like background noise. He does not wish to compete with outside influences. Instead, He wants and deserves to have our undivided attention. Why? He wants us to be able to hear Him. We cannot hear Him if we hear everything else around us.

When I go into my room and pray, I not only shut the door, I also lock the door. This ensures that my time with the Lord will not be interrupted, that my family will not barge in while I am in the midst of deep prayer with the Lord. My family also knows that when I am praying and the door is locked, they should not disturb me. I also turn off my cell phone, the radio, television, etc. In that moment, I am not reachable by the outside world, and I am fully able to focus on the Lord. Be assured, the steps that we take to ensure privacy with the Lord also greatly please the Lord, and He too will honor our privacy with Him.

Second, we are told by the Lord to pray to our Father. Jesus Himself cried, "Abba, Father." We are to have an intimate relationship with God the Father. In Matthew 6:8 (NIV) we are told by Jesus that our *"…Father knows what you need before you ask Him."* God the Father knows what we need before we ask Him. But it is in the asking of Him that the intimacy comes. How does a child come before a loving father? He comes and sits upon his knee. He is not afraid to ask anything of him, for he knows that his father knows what is best for him and will provide for him. In the same way, we are to come before our heavenly Father. We are to sit upon His knee. He desires us to ask of Him, believing that He will provide for us all of our needs. We also come before Him with reverence and humility. Just as we respected our earthly fathers, we are to respect and revere our heavenly Father. It is in this time of intimacy with the Father that the Father reveals His heart to us.

Third, it is in the Secret Place with Him that we become who we are to become for the Kingdom of God. To be a world-changer we must understand our identity in God and know who we are in Him as well as our purpose in the Kingdom. It is here in the Secret Place where we are taught by the Lord, trained by the Lord, comforted by the Lord, loved by the Lord. Yes, we can go to conferences, listen to tapes, and read books, but the real transformation in us takes place in the Secret Place with the Lord. For it is here that we weep. It is here that we laugh. It is here that we obey. It is here that we submit. It is here that we die to ourselves. It is here that we begin to dream. It is here that He reveals His will to us. It is here that He first commissions us. It is here that He encourages us. It is here that we become the world-changer that we are to become. It is here in the Secret Place that the Lord reveals to us the work of the Kingdom that we are to do.

Jesus said in John 5:17 (NIV): *"My Father is always at His work to this very day, and I, too, am working."* The Lord is always working. We are to be working too; however, we are to do only that which the Lord desires us to do. How do we know what we are to do? We know what we are to do by spending time with Him. When we spend time with Him, He clarifies our call, our direction, and with the help of the Holy Spirit guides us each step of the way down the path that He has us on to reach our divine destiny in Him.

The problem in the Body of Christ today is that people want to go from A to Z immediately. They do not understand that God is about process. We must allow Him to process us. We must continually submit to His process, even though at times we may not like it. We must fully commit to His process in us. World-changers are not made overnight, but instead like fine wine or fine food there is a process that takes place within them. It is God's process in us. That process is also uniquely different for each child of God. My call and purpose is not the same as yours; my process is also not the same as yours. It is in the Secret Place where we learn to submit to His process. This is done on a daily basis. It is in the Secret Place where we learn to die to what are our own desires, and not His desires for us. It is in the Secret Place where we make His desires ours and where we fully embrace His plan for our lives.

In the Secret Place the Lord also comforts us, consoles us, teaches us, corrects us, and ministers to us in many ways through the Person of the Holy Spirit. He often speaks to me in the Secret Place in prayer through visions, acrostics, and poetry. I have learned many things from the Lord while in the Secret Place. I have learned that the Lord knows each of us intimately and everything about us. He knows our sins before we confess them. He knows what words we are going to say in prayer even before we utter them. The Lord sometimes will finish my sentences for me, for He knows the words even before I speak them out of my mouth. He knows what we are struggling with and what we have overcome. He loves us deeply, and He desires for us to passionately pursue Him and worship Him with all of our being.

He recently has been teaching me much about humility. He greatly desires and will have humility in His people and especially in His Bride. He said to me, "The degree to which one humbles himself or herself before My servants reveals to Me and to others the degree to which he or she is humble before Me. For those who are humble before Me will also be humble before My servants." The term "My servants" here means other Christians. We are to be humble before other Christians. This is not always easy, but it is necessary for our spiritual growth. He also places us in situations where we can see and gauge our own humility. This is for our benefit, not His, for He already knows where we are.

For example, I was recently at a ministry meeting where there were several other pastors and leaders present. I knew many of the other pastors and leaders who were in the room. The speaker had a word of knowledge that I knew was for me. I had never heard this particular speaker before, nor had he ever prayed for me before. I knew though that the Holy Spirit had something for me and was prompting me. I did not want to ignore His leading. I knew that I needed to go forward for prayer. I knew that I had to humble myself and receive from the speaker and also from the Lord. The Lord honored my humility and gave me a beautiful word that touched me deeply. I was the only pastor or leader who went forward that day. When I asked the Lord about this later that day, during my time with Him in the Secret Place, He told me what I have previously shared above regarding the need for the Body of Christ to be humble before His servants as well as before Him. For He is constantly speaking to us, if we will only hear Him, obey Him, and have a heart of humility before Him.

## Points to Ponder

1. Do you have a Secret Place alone with the Lord? If not, what is holding you back? Take some time today to spend alone with God. Start with ten minutes, and gradually increase your time each day. It is OK if you do not spend a lot of time at first. What matters is that you spend time with Him. Soon, you will enjoy your Secret Place so much that you will not want to leave, and minutes will turn easily and quickly into hours with Him.

2. What is the Lord revealing to you in your Secret Place about your call and your work in His Kingdom? What are you to be doing today? this week? this month? in the next six months? this year?

3. Where are you in God's processing of you? Have you submitted to His process, or are you fighting against His process? Be honest with yourself. The Lord loves honesty. It is refreshing to Him. Confess to Him and ask for forgiveness of any sins that may be holding you back in His process within you.

4. Have you embraced His plan for your life, at least to the extent that He has revealed it to you? If not, what is holding you back?

These are hard questions to ask ourselves, but they are, nonetheless, questions that must be asked. For to be a world-changer, we need to commit to going all the way with the

Lord. That takes place in the intimacy of the Secret Place with Him. It is here that we choose to be a world-changer or not. It is here that we say "yes" or "no" to Him. It is here that we make the crucial choices regarding our lives and our relationship with Him that impact our destiny not only in earth but also in Heaven.

# CHAPTER 11

# A Powerful Eruption

## Susan East

*And from the days of John the Baptist until now the kingdom of heaven suffereth violence, and the violent take it by force* (Matthew 11:12 KJV).

*"And the violent take it by force!"* This phrase sums up our Kingdom mandate. It is the means by which we take possession of our Kingdom promises. Like John the Baptist, we must live our lives in obedience with no compromise for the furtherance of the Kingdom and the Glory of the One who was and is and is to come. We also must speak powerfully, boldly, and intently, for the Kingdom of God is at hand. We must resonate as the forceful eruption of the reality of the Kingdom of God in the midst of the nations. We must be willing to declare with all honesty, "Here am I! Send me!"

We must be ready, willing, and able to be molded into faithful and valiant servants of the Living God, setting our faces like flint. As we sacrifice our self-control, we are submitting ourselves fully to the "Commander in Chief" of the heavenly forces, thus eradicating double-mindedness. As we are driven by an intense passion for His abiding presence, we become extremely fierce Kingdom warriors demonstrating the Kingdom of Heaven erupting forcefully, and becoming the forceful who are seizing it.

In this season, there is a great rising up taking place within God's people, resulting in circumcision of hearts. A "trustworthy leadership" is emerging that displays a holy and reverent attitude in regards to God's Word and in the building up of His Body! This is rectifying the cycle of abuse of authority within the church, which has caused God's children to become disillusioned by those in leadership. In the past, many have focused on "men of stature" instead of Jesus. The earthly vessel is the conduit for the administering of God's Word, but the Holy Spirit is the Teacher of God's Truth.

We must willfully submit to our wilderness experience. This process strips us of all carnal thoughts and emotions. This is the place where our minds are renewed and transformed into the mind of Christ. Just like Moses, we will feel utterly exiled and forsaken without a country and without hope! During the turmoil of the dark night of the soul, we will experience helplessness, adversity, and loneliness. With the fury of the taskmaster's whip, the hot desert winds will blow the blinding sands into our eyes. However, we must stand firm while moving forward to possess a land unseen, a kingdom not yet perceived!

Prophets are cleansed and purged for God's ordained purpose in this crucible of despair. We do not have control over the force within us that drives us onward through the place of fear and doubt where our fleshly strength falters. In this place we are beaten into the dust from which we were created and we are forged into swords by God's hand. This journey takes us back to the life-giving water of renewing and refreshing where we partake of the River of Life that flows from the Rock, Jesus.

There is a contending for those entering into the Kingdom of Heaven. Since the Kingdom suffers a holy violence, we must strive, run, wrestle, and fight to press through to win the prize. We will encounter opposition from both without and within. With a strong desire, we will not quit nor let go without receiving the blessing of rest for those who labor. The Kingdom is always under attack in both the natural and in the spirit. We engage in warfare with three enemies: the world, the flesh, and the enemy of our souls. Choosing to do what we know is righteous goes against the grain of our fallen human nature. The violence occurs as we uproot all that is not of God in our lives, positioning us to receive God's grace. As we receive God's grace, it enables us to be loosed into uprooting the issues in our lives. This position then allows God's character to be built in us, for without character we can never properly possess or advance the Kingdom.

There are different levels and kinds of grace. Grace must precede everything else, for by His grace we are saved, live, breathe, and have our very being. Our alignment with His grace becomes our level of submission to the process of building His character in us. Thus when we make the effort to do what we know is well-pleasing to God, we align ourselves properly to receive the favor and grace of God.

Since the Kingdom of God has many layers of divine mysteries, we must view it from various perspectives. The full expression of the Kingdom bursts forth full of power and life as it is advanced. The vibrant power of love is the violent force that enables us to attain the Kingdom. As the holy fire of God's love is kindled, it burns higher and higher when our passion is re-focused on the things of God as the things of earth become strangely dim.

The foundation of Kingdom violence is rooted in the purification process that results in death to self. Out of that place of death arises a holy passion and an intimate relationship with Abba, Father. The violent will persevere and triumph over all evil forces to take hold of the Kingdom of Heaven. We can truly say: "I am my Beloved's and He is mine"!

We must not permit anything to deter us from our desire to seek and find the Lord with all our hearts, all our souls, and all our strength. We must check our heart's intent and justify our priorities accordingly. The fervent burning and yearning of our hearts will become one with the burning love of Christ as the River of Life flows into us from His pierced side. When He becomes our All in All, that is when we have seized the Kingdom by force!

A few months ago I was part of a gathering where several worshipers who previously did not know one another came together for a time of spontaneous worship. As we entered into worship in unison, each person offered his or her particular act of worship unto the Lord. Psalmists, dancers, vocalists, and musicians proclaimed, danced, sang, and played various instruments, all in tune to the Holy Spirit. During this time we also experienced moments of silence, spontaneous eruptions of both joy and weeping, and spiritual birthing. We entered into a very deep place as we touched Heaven to the degree of changing earth. We stepped into the realm of "on earth as it is in Heaven." It definitely was a time for all flesh to be stripped away with the intent of touching the Father's heart.

As I was driving down the interstate on my way home after the gathering dispersed, the Holy Spirit spoke the following to me during the midnight hour: "Convergence of the sons of Zadok and the sons of Issachar." Then I heard simultaneously: "They knew the times and the seasons." "The time is upon us when true worshipers shall worship the Father in spirit and in truth." As these words resonated in my spirit, the Holy Spirit continued to download to me more of the Word of God pertaining to this.

Zadok's name means "righteous, just, or to make right in a moral sense."[1] Zadok and his sons were priests with great integrity who were deeply committed to the call of God on their lives to worship Him. They were sanctified, consecrated, and called to draw near to and worship God Himself. The sons of Zadok had a vertical worship. They worshiped upward to God. Vertical ministry is a unique and a very high call to God Himself. Under the Zadok anointing you will find release as you soar upward into the throne room and become lost in His presence. This is the place where the fear of man stops, as you experience realms of His Spirit. In this anointing you will see visions, hear heavenly sounds, and find healing and miracles begin to flow. Zadok worship will lift you higher and higher as you climb the Mount of Ascension, where He becomes the very center of your being as you fall before His throne. This is the place of true union of God and man, where satisfaction with the worship is reached with man as well as God.

The Zadok anointing is given by God and comes from the spirit of a man being touched by the Spirit of God. Its purpose is to minister to God, but you will be ministered to as well. It is about the awesome presence of God as He Himself is drawn to His people by true spiritual worship. As God speaks to His people through the prophetic words of new songs, a new sound is released into the atmosphere through this anointing.

Issachar's name means "he will bring a reward, or man for hire."[2] Those who walk by the virtue of Issachar walk in his character and calling to bring a reward to the Lord as well as to the harvest field in which they are working. They are able to distinguish between that which is wise and unwise and pursue the understanding needed to live holy before the Lord. This understanding comes from the Lord Himself, since they know God in an intimate manner. Because they walk in wisdom, Issachars are able to perceive and seize the moment of opportunity for success and wealth. They walk in revelatory understanding birthed through intimacy with the Lord, and their words possess great power and authority.

Issachar embraced the character of God to the point that his soulish nature was consumed. There must be nothing left of flesh, only God, enabling us to stand before the fiery God and behold His everlasting beauty. When we embrace death to self to become alive to God, revelation is released to us to understand the times and seasons. When we operate in that place of obedience, giving ourselves over to God, we are prompted to follow and obey Him. It is a wise choice to rest in the Lord and have an intimate bride/bridegroom relationship with Him. Our vision should be for the Lord Himself and His harvest field, the delightful nations upon whose fields are "white for harvest."

Issachar found rest and strength in the secret place with the Lord and was worthy of the call to shoulder burdens. Throughout Scripture we see that the shoulder represents carrying a burden of some type and also represents different realms of authority and responsibility. Because of his radical obedience, Issachar was a humble burden-bearer and a willing servant. He gained authority over disobedience, never giving up, not even under the strain of potential loss of life. He did not permit sickness or weariness to distract him from focusing on God. He operated by the Spirit of the Lord, not in his own power and might, and loved not his life even unto death.

God values the Issachar anointing to the degree that He called all of us to function in it, whether to bear His burden in a governmental or shepherding arena, or to bear His burden for the harvest. God wants us to understand the times and what needs to be done in the midst of each situation and season, regardless of what our individual burdens are. Vision and counsel combine to bring the understanding of times and the knowledge of what to do to put the plans of God in proper perspective. Every vineyard is in need of this anointing to enable the people to prosper in their mission. God's wisdom and understanding enrich the work of the vineyard, bringing revelation to prosper and become abundantly fruitful fields.

When we roll our burdens onto the Lord, we take up the Lord's yoke, not our own. This is a picture of the costliness of intercession, the model and source being found in Christ. We must also choose to be of no reputation, and take upon us the form of a servant, humble ourselves, and become obedient unto death.

In our perception of God's seasons, we must realize that God in His wisdom has His own priorities to prepare the ground for the next timetable. God will do nothing without first revealing it to His prophets who possess an intimate relationship with Him. This is a season to buy oil, to keep our lamps full and our wicks trimmed. We must know the time and the season to know the purpose of God, so we can co-labor with Christ effectively. Obedience is better than sacrifice. Jesus only did what He saw the Father doing and only said what He heard the Father saying. We cannot afford to operate by might, power, or in the flesh in these days, but only by His Holy Spirit!

Those who violently praise, worship, and intercede in prayer will tear through the thin veil that separates the heavenly Kingdom from the earthly realm. A habitation of God's presence will manifest "on earth as it is in Heaven"!

It is due time for the Worship Warriors to *arise*! As we begin to exercise the authority Jesus gave to us, we will break through the heavens into the heart of God. As we are obedient, He will give us the revelation that will enable us to accomplish His will and change the atmosphere around us. As we seek God's face in worship, He will instill a great passion in us. We need to become so desperate and undone that our hunger for seeking and finding more and more of God's face cannot be satisfied. As we are faithful to pursue the One who is actually chasing us, we will enter the Kingdom dimension by way of which we have never passed before.

As we ascend in worship and come boldly into our Father's throne room, we will be connected with God in the most powerful and supernatural way. As we begin to walk in this new level of victory, we receive a deeper revelation of God's will and plan. As we are drawn out of the world's pattern, we are transformed into being what God created us to be at the foundations of creation. From this place we begin to view things from a heavenly perspective. The Holy Spirit is revealed to us as the Comforter in the midst of all of our trials and tribulations. As we enter into this new Kingdom realm, God opens the door for His presence and power to invade the earth. As our faith arises to a new level, the promises of God become realities in our lives.

As we give God our time and continually express our hearts in worship, we release a sound that beckons a response from the earth. There is a power and frequency dispersed as we join to lift our voices in worship to the living God. True worship is an abiding place that is as natural as breathing. In this place we can express our adoration for Him in various ways: We can stand, lift our hands in worship, clap our hands, bow, kneel, or dance. We can speak, shout, sing, or play instruments. We can be silent, quiet, or loud. We can weep, travail, or experience birth pangs. As we express our hearts to God, we posture ourselves to be passionate worshipers before Him.

As spiritual warfare is increasing, the Holy Spirit is training us to ascend in worship so that we can learn to descend in war. Yesterday's manna is no longer adequate for the day we are now in. As a new level of spirituality rises up within us, we ascend into our Father's throne room where our own understanding no longer makes sense. Because the weapons of our warfare are not carnal but mighty for the pulling down of strongholds, He releases heavenly revelation to us that enables us to fight to victory from a position of worship.

God has given us authority and incredible power to break the strongholds of the enemy on earth. Through prayer and worship we break through the second heaven into the third Heaven, where we are surrounded by God's presence. In His presence we are equipped for war, and the enemy's strategies come to utter destruction. As we walk in peace, we poise ourselves to listen and hear God's voice. When we are in the place of peace that passes all understanding, we find revelation, insight, and strategy to hold our ground in the situation in which we find ourselves.

As our faith arises to a new level, we begin to believe and expect God to speak to us personally and reveal heavenly knowledge. Pressing on through with persistence is the method of taking back new ground. As we continue to overcome, God will give us new insight and bring us into new places of ongoing warfare. Worship and praise is the key that unlocks victory as we enter uncharted battlegrounds. We are in preparation for taking the Kingdom by force. In this season of warfare and worship, change and conflict birth the harvest. Let us go forth proclaiming: "Behold, the Kingdom of God is at hand."

As we step into the authority and power of our God-given positions, we will be rooted and grounded in His footprints of stability. We will be akin to those who once turned the world upside down after Christ's resurrection. For as a seed must fall to the ground and die for new life to be brought forth, so He also had to go away in order for the Comforter to be sent to lead us in all truth.

We are in the process of *becoming* "world-changers" as we continue to preach the Gospel of the Kingdom. We do not only speak forth in Jesus' name, but we also must emanate all of His attributes and attitudes in thought, word, and deed. We must exhibit and radiate the unconditional love of God for the lost world to see Jesus in and through our eyes, which are the windows to our hearts and souls.

As we go forth preaching the Gospel of the Kingdom to the poor, we can rest in Jesus' promise to us that *"greater things than these will we do"* (see John 14:12). We will become conduits through which the power of the blood and stripes of Jesus will cause the demons to flee, the blind to see, the lame to walk, the lepers to be cleansed, the deaf to hear, and the dead to be raised.

It is time to go outside the four walls and begin to demonstrate the Kingdom of God as the power of the Holy Spirit flows through and out of us in signs, wonders, and miracles! Go forth boldly in obedience and compassion. As ambassadors of Christ, capture hearts that lead to the salvation of souls.

May the light of Christ, the Hope of Glory rise up within us and permeate and pierce the surrounding darkness. See the lost sheep through Jesus' eyes of compassion, and may they see Jesus' love in and through our eyes! Keep in tune to hear the Father's voice with precision accuracy so that they may be drawn to the Father through our voice, the Living Word Spoken that will not return void but will accomplish that purpose which it was sent out to accomplish!

## Points to Ponder

1. Is your heart's desire to enter into a deeper relationship with God?

2. Are you willing to release to God the things that hold you back from serving and seeking Him with all your might?

3. Have you experienced the Father in an intimate way?

4. Do you long to be a worshiper who abides in His presence?

5. Will you say, "Yes, Lord," to the refining process that will mold you into a violent Kingdom Taker?

## Endnotes

1. Zadok meaning; http://www.hyperdictionary.com/dictionary/ZADOK; accessed October 11, 2010.

2. Encarta® World English Dictionary [North American Edition] © & (P) 2009 Microsoft Corporation. All rights reserved. Developed for Microsoft by Bloomsbury Publishing Plc.

# CHAPTER 12

# Open the Door

## Jim Wilbur

Not too long ago I picked up a book that has been on my bookshelf for quite some time. The title of the book is *A Passion for Fullness,* and it is written by Jack Hayford. As I began to flip through that book, the following arrested me and has not let me go since:

> The greatest monster threatening abounding fruitfulness [Fullness] in my life…isn't lust, greed, conceit, or error; it's the unperceived smugness that drugs the soul with the notion that our boundaries of understanding God are the boundaries of His readiness to reveal Himself to us…He isn't asking us if we think we know everything…He's asking how much are we willing to receive of Him—of the newness of His Spirit today![1]

As I read that I was acutely aware that over the past several years my smugness wasn't only unperceived by me, but it was obnoxiously apparent to everyone else. I had somehow decided that I needed to be the authority on everything and, in the process, lost my pathway to His presence. I had unknowingly boxed God in and decided that He didn't need to move any more than I needed Him to. The problem is that God does not respect my boxes. As a matter of fact, the last time He was in a box, if you touched it, you would die.

If you were or are like me, I have good news! There is an antidote that carries the cure for a smug soul. It is the antidote of awareness that freed my soul and opened my eyes to see and taste that the Lord is still always good! The Father is merciful and kind and in our smugness He can and will interrupt it with His truth. When He does, it is just like a veil being removed from your eyes to see what has been there all along.

Several months ago during a time of prayer I had one of those veils removed. God gave me a picture of a door that separated two rooms. He said to me that the door represented prayer and the two rooms were representative of my heart and the throne room of Heaven. As the door was kept open, a river of gold flowed freely back and forth from room to room. I asked the Father, "What is keeping the door open?" He said, "The doorstop is awareness." As long as the door was kept open, the river flowed freely and without restriction.

Later I asked what the substance was, and the Holy Spirit told me it was "His glory, and within His glory (nature and character) was communion (communication) from the throne room of Heaven." As His glory flowed freely from His throne room to my heart it would then saturate my soul (mind, will, and emotions), shaping me to be more and more like Him. As His glory filled my soul, it would begin to pour over the edges and touch others around me.

## "When the Door Is Open, Nothing Can Stop the Flow"

Those are the words that the Father said to me next and I pondered this for quite some time. A few days later as I was driving and listening to worship music, I heard the still small voice of the Holy Spirit say to me, "Play that again and again." I pushed repeat, and as I did had a wonderful and powerful experience with the love of God.

The Holy Spirit then said to me, "I am renewing your mind about My love." I then realized that there are many ways that the Father can and will change me into His image and likeness. As my mind is being renewed into becoming more like Him and my capacity is being enlarged to carry His fullness, it is my awareness of who He is and how He feels about me that empowers me to live, move, and have my being in the reality of His fullness. The truth is that every believer has been given access to the store rooms of Heaven that are without boundary and have a limitless supply.

*To know the love of Christ which passes knowledge; that you may be filled with all the fullness of God* (Ephesians 3:19 NKJV).

This verse says to me that when I am aware of the love of God, the reality of that love supersedes anything I have ever learned or experienced this side of Heaven. In that reality I have my capacity enlarged to carry everything that is needed to see the dream that the Father has placed inside of me fulfilled. It is the awareness that awakens my heart and allows me to see and hear what the Father is saying and doing. A.W. Tozer defined it as: "A habitual conscious communion" with God.[2]

When I am aware of this love, I do not have to strive or work my way into His presence. I can just go, and so can you. In Ephesians 3:12 Paul tells us that it is our faith that gives us access to the Father with freedom and without fear. When I live my life in awareness of the Father's love, I am able to see things from His perspective and not mine. I am empowered to see others as He sees them and to speak into that reality until they can dare begin to see the same way.

When I set my heart and mind to focus on things that are above I am able to gain a different perspective because my focus and attention is on the eternal and not the temporal.

When I fix my eyes on Jesus, I am able to see the solution, and the problems just seem to fade into the background.

*Since, then, you have been raised with Christ, set your heart on things above, where Christ is seated at the right hand of God. Set your minds on things above, not on earthly things. For you died, and your life is hidden with Christ in God* (Colossians 3:1-3 NIV).

When I have become aware and gained this perspective, I am able to enter freely into the presence of God and experience what the apostle Paul describes as continual prayer.

*Pray continually, give thanks in all circumstances; for this is God's will for you in Christ Jesus* (1 Thessalonians 5:17-18 NIV).

This awareness allows me to look completely differently at prayer. One of the most simple and profound definitions of prayer I have ever read is from Madame Guyon in the classic book, *Experiencing God Through Prayer*. Guyon states that prayer is "nothing more than turning our heart toward God and receiving in turn His love."[3] It is when I set my heart to pursue God that I am now positioned to receive His unconditional love and give it away to the very next person that I meet.

I can think of so many different times in my life that this very awareness of the presence and the love of the Father has unlocked my heart and allowed for God to complete a deep work within my soul. I would like to share with you one of the most significant times that this happened. It was simple words that led to profound change.

In 2001, I was asked to attend a conference named "The Father Loves You." I thought to myself, *I know God loves me,* but agreed to go because I was sure I could learn something that would help me as I ministered to others.

During the conference all the pastors and leaders were asked to come up front for prayer, and I was desperate for prayer and wasted no time bolting to the front. As the conference speaker and several other people walked down the long row of pastors and leaders assembled there from all around the world, I witnessed God moving in powerful ways. Many of those prayed for were "visibly" touched by the presence of God.

As the conference speakers and prayer team approached me, they began to pray and "nothing" happened. I remember thinking, *What is wrong with me?* and I just kept standing there. It is important to understand that this was a power-packed bunch of leaders and teachers who are known worldwide for their powerful ministries, and I was "just standing there." I kept thinking there must be something wrong with me. As they finished praying for me, I was grateful but a little frustrated, to say the least, that nothing had happened.

I had just about given up when one of the prayer team members came up to me and put his hand in mine and in a soft voice said to me, "God is willing to give you much more than you are willing to receive." The person only said it once, but that is all it took and I immediately was aware of the presence of God and was able to hear His internal voice speak to my heart: "Jim, you don't trust Me."

I answered back, "Yes, I do. You are my Savior."

Then God replied back internally and said, "You don't trust Me with your whole heart."

And at that moment I knew that God was right, but as I became aware I was determined to do something about it. Those simple words were the key that opened up my heart and in the next few days allowed me to experience a deep revelation of the Father's love that has transformed my life, family, and ministry. As soon as I became **aware** that God was *for* me and not *against* me, it opened the door to enter into His presence and receive His love into the deep places of my heart that had been locked up tight for years.

Fellow world-changers, I would like to leave you with this statement as you pursue God and seek to understand His ways:

*Awareness of His love allows me to enter into His presence with freedom and without fear. The truth is, He is for you and not against you! Let's go turn the world upside down!*

## Points to Ponder

1. When was the last time that you took a few minutes to think about how the Father really sees you? Take some time now and write down what He tells you.

2. Is it possible that when I know who I am in Christ, I can see other people differently? Today as you are living life, ask the Father to show you the Glory in the people around you.

3. Research the Scriptures and write out those Scriptures that speak to who you are and the dream that God has placed inside of you. Take those Scriptures and spend time meditating on them. Write down what the Father tells you.

## Endnotes

1. Jack Hayford, *A Passion for Fullness* (Fort Worth, TX: Life Publishing, 1990), 3.

2. A.W. Tozer, *The Pursuit of God* (Harrisburg, PA: Christian Publications, 1948), n.p.

3. Madame Jean Guyon, *Experiencing God Through Prayer* (Springdale, PA: Whitaker House, 1984), 11.

# More About the Authors

**Don Nori Sr.**

Don Nori has authored eight books and has worked in the publishing industry for more than 25 years. He has ministered internationally for more than two decades, working with people of all races and nationalities. Don and his wife of 35 years, Cathy, live at the foot of the Appalachian Mountains in south-central Pennsylvania where they raised five sons and now also enjoy daughters-in-law and grandchildren.

**Patricia King**

Patricia King is a passionate, prophetic personality who is the host of Extreme Prophetic Television. She has had over 25 years of background as a Christian minister in conference speaking, prophetic service, church leadership, and television and radio appearances. Patricia is an author of books, booklets, and manuals and has produced many informative resources through the media of tapes, videos, CDs, and DVDs. Her reputation in the Christian community is world-renowned. You will find her to be sincere, genuine, generous, honest, and real.

**D.M. Collins**

A lifelong Word-lover and encourager, D.M. Collins is passionate to see God's people cleaned up, healed up, and trained up to live out their primary mission: to love one another as Jesus loves us and to take that heart-changing Love into all the world.

**Rob Coscia**

Rob Coscia and his wife Angi have been in ministry for 20 years. They are presently the lead pastors of Diamond Valley Church, a church plant in Dallas, Pennsylvania. Rob is ordained with Global Awakening under Randy Clark. Rob was educated at Wilkes University in Wilkes-Barre, Pennsylvania, with majors in political science and history, and at North Central University in Minneapolis, Minnesota. Rob's passion is to see people equipped and trained to live at the full capacity of what Jesus has made possible. Rob and Angi have two amazing children: Kim, 19, and Rob, 18.

**Barbie Breathitt**

Dr. Barbie Breathitt is an author, ordained minister, dedicated educator, and respected teacher of the supernatural manifestations of God. Barbie's dynamic teaching skills, intelligence, and quick wit keep her a favorite with audiences everywhere. Through prayer, intense study, and years of research, Barbie has become a recognized leader in dream interpretation and has equipped people in more than 40 nations around the globe. Her prophetic gifting and deep spiritual insights have helped thousands of people understand the supernatural ways God speaks to us today.

**Adam LiVecchi**

Adam LiVecchi and his beautiful wife Sarah are the founders of We See Jesus Ministries. It is an itinerant ministry that focuses on equipping, imparting, and activating the saints for the work of the ministry. The desire of We See Jesus Ministries is to see the church conformed to the image of Christ and to see the church manifest Jesus to the world that so desperately needs Him. They teach and impart the ministry of healing, and also help people learn how to develop a lifestyle of hearing the voice of God and obeying. For more information go to: www.weseejesusministries.com.

**Abby Abildness**

Abby Abildness is the founder and president of Healing Tree International in Hershey, Pennsylvania, and she is the Aglow International Lighthouse President of the Hershey Area Aglow Community Lighthouse. She is an ordained pastor with Life Center Ministries International of Harvest International Ministries, and a Marriage and Family Therapist. She is the Pennsylvania Representative for Cindy Jacobs Reformation Prayer Network and John Benefiel's Heartland Ministries Apostolic Network. She is a former Behavioral Science professor at Penn State University Hershey Medical Center, and Pastoral Care professor at Myerstown Theological Seminary. She and her husband, Dr. James Abildness, have four children and two grandchildren.

**1**

**Dorsey Marshall**

Dorsey Marshall has been serving in ministry for more than 50 years and is involved in church planting in the United States, India, and currently in the West Indies. He and Pat have been married more than 48 years and are living on Maryland's Delmarva Peninsula near the beautiful Chesapeake Bay where they raised their two sons, and now enjoy daughters-in-law and four wonderful grandchildren. He has authored a daily devotional, *The Success Minute*, for the past 15 years, which touches five continents of the earth.

**Doug Alexander**

Doug Alexander first met the Lord in 1984. He's a master's level, licensed substance abuse counselor. Through his ministry, Morning Dew Therapy, he specializes in helping at-risk youth caught up in drugs and gangs. Doug lives in Mesa, Arizona, with his wife Amy and two precious daughters: Johannah and Cassidy.

**Lisa Jo Greer**

Lisa Jo Greer is president and founder of Awake The Bride Ministries. An ordained minister, she desires to see the Body move into a deeper, more intimate and passionate relationship with the Lord, and to be the Bride that it is called to be. Lisa graduated *magna cum laude* from the Evangelical School of Theology and holds a M.A.R. degree in Old Testament, New Testament, and Theology. She is also a member of the Christian International Apostolic Network and the Association of Bridge Churches. She is author of the book, *The Preparation Realm of Heaven*. Lisa resides in Grantham, Pennsylvania, with her husband and daughter.

**Susan East**

Susan East is founder of Zarapheth Ministries, whose commission is based on First Kings 17. Descended from one of the first purchasers of land in Pennsylvania whose signature was first on the original Pennsylvania charter, Susan's family heritage is that of a "Forerunner." Her passion is to "Know Christ and let Him be known." She is an intercessor, worshiper, and warrior. Susan resides in Waynesboro, Pennsylvania, near her three children and three grandchildren.

**Jim Wilbur**

Dr. Jim Wilbur and his wife, Christie, are the founders of No Limit Ministries and have a passion to communicate the heart of the Father to the world. They live in Kingston, Pennsylvania, and have three incredible boys who keep them on their toes. Jim received his Doctor of Ministry from Vision International University after serving 12 years in the United States Army. Jim is currently serving as the Executive Chaplain of Providing Hope Ministries—whose primary mission is to provide chaplaincy care to the Luzerne County Correctional Facility, Wilkes-Barre, Pennsylvania. To learn more please visit www.reach2dream.blogspot.com.

# *Notes*

So You Want to Change the World?

_____

_____

_____

_____

_____

_____

_____

_____

_____

_____

_____

_____

_____

_____

_____

_____

_____

_____

_____

_____

*Notes*

# So You Want to Change the World?

_____

_____

_____

_____

_____

_____

_____

_____

_____

_____

_____

_____

_____

_____

_____

_____

_____

_____

_____

_____

_____

_____

_____

_____

*Notes*

_____
_____
_____
_____
_____
_____
_____
_____
_____
_____
_____
_____
_____
_____
_____
_____
_____
_____
_____
_____
_____
_____
_____
_____

*Notes*